The Magic of Aesop

*How to Use the Wisdom of Aesop's Fables
to Spark Your Transformational Change*

Robert Martel

MagicofAesop.com

The Magic of Aesop

How to Use the Wisdom of Aesop's Fables to Spark Your Transformational Change

ISBN 978-1-7354770-0-8
Library of Congress Catalog Number 2020914222
First printing: August 2020

Positive Results Hypnosis
www.positiveresultshypnosis.com
www.magicofaesop.com
(508) 733-1868

Cover Design by Bogdan Matei

Robert Martel is available to speak at your business or conference event on a variety of topics. Call (508) 481-8383 for more information or send an email to bob@bobmartel.com

This book is dedicated to who else, but to Aesop and his master Xanthus. And perhaps Phaedrus, Herodotus, Aristophanes and Apollonius. Honorable mention to Maximus Planudes for writing the biography of Aesop as well as the first prose versions of his fables. Milton H. Erickson, Ben Edwin Perry, and William Caxton each deserve a nod as well!

Of course, I dedicate this book to Lori, for her encouragement and support.

"... like those who dine well of the plainest dishes,
Aesop made use of humble incidents to teach great truths;
by announcing a story which everyone knows not to be true,
he told the truth by the very fact that he did not
claim to be relating real events."

Philostratus, The Life of Apollonius of Tyana, Book V:14

Praise for The Magic of Aesop
(What readers are saying)

"The Magic of Aesop is a delightful text for therapists or really anyone who uses story to teach and cause change in others. The return to Aesop is to remind all therapists the value in the centuries, long tradition of Aesop. Martel collects behavioral science, Ericksonian hypnotic techniques and touches of NLP here and there to give story tellers a new set of brushes to set next to their toolbox. I enjoyed the book, found ancient ideas brought forth in a new light and credit Bob Martel with doing a service while adding to the literature of hypnotic storytelling. Certainly, you'll want this on your bookshelf today." -Kevin Hogan, PsyD Author *of The New Hypnotherapy Handbook, The Science of Influence and The Psychology of Persuasion*

"This book provides not only insights into ancient fables but is also creates a roadmap in using the wisdom of Aesop in helping to change lives. Martel has done a masterful job in sharing his Aesopian style of hypnosis work. Everyone in the change work profession ought to read this book."

- Richard Nongard,
Professional Hypnotist and author of Viral Leadership, Speak Ericksonian, The Seven Most Effective Methods of Self Hypnosis and many more.

"Each of us assigns value to the stories we hear throughout our lives. Hypnotic storytelling is powerful in affecting change in the mind of the client, as this book reveals. The morals of Aesop's Fables are magical, and Bob has done an excellent job of introducing the value Aesop to the clinical hypnotic process. Through selected fables Bob shares how he uses the fables to assist the client in making great strides toward their goal progress. He makes it easy for anyone working with others to expertly introduce the fables of Aesop to their change work!"

- Jason Linett,
Hypnotist, Author of Work Smart Business

"The Magic of Aesop takes a fresh look at the power and wisdom of the stories contained in the fables we all grew up with. Bob Martel lays out clearly the path of fables and how they have been used as a passive teaching method for 100's of years. What better way to teach people than to let them teach themselves! With this ground-breaking book, Mr. Martel explains how you as a hypnotherapist can use the power of fables, to enhance your hypnotherapy practice and reach deeper levels of acceptance with your clients to help them reach their goals. A new modality to add to your tool chest. Finally, Bob explains how you too, can write your own fables and how they can be used not only in a clinical setting but as a tool for individuals and businesses to get their message out. Highly recommended for anyone interested in deepening and differentiating themselves in the market and wanting to get their message out in a non-obtrusive, gentle way."

- Thomas Roman,
Entreprenuer, The Quantum Group

"Bob has provided the very book of fables I have been looking for since I started my hypnosis career. If you are a hypnotic storyteller this is a must have for your collection, and if you have not yet added hypnotic storytelling to your change work, this book is a must read! Interesting facts and fun to read thanks and praise to Bob for a job well done." -Anthony Gitch, Hypnotist, Author of The Art of Self Destruction

"Bob is a true fabulist, himself. His love of storytelling to help others, and his ability to comprehend how a good story can help make shifts in an individual at a deep level comes through in this book. Filled with a fascinating history and stories of Aesop and fellow fabulists, as well as fables themselves, the book itself is spellbinding and hard to put down, This book is truly a fabulous resource for anyone in a role of influencing or helping others."

- Kevin Martin,
Master Hypnotist, author of Living Your Dream Life

This is the most significant and exciting book for hypnotherapists that I have read in a long time. I'm always looking for new ways of creating metaphors. I love how you teach the reader in your scripts. I've stared at my copy of Aesop's Fables many times and known that its packed full of gems. This book is filled with powerful storytelling techniques which makes it useful as a continuing reference."

- Roger Moore,
Institute of Hypnotherapy

"In the Magic of Aesop Bob Martel show us how the fables of Aesop use the animal world to reveal timeless truths that throw light on the human condition. He describes how you can use the magical power of fable in your practice as a tool to help your clients see life from a different perspective so they understand the deeper meaning and message that's being presented to them. Not only that, but he teaches you how to create your own fables that will inspire your clients to make changes. It's a book full of wisdom and knowledge that will be an asset to any hypnotist in helping clients to make progress."

- Maggie Dennison,
Mindset and Marketing Coach

"You are about to embark on a great book by a gifted author. Bob Martel will take you on a journey as Aesop has through the Centuries of many lives. As Aesop did, Bob Martel will teach you to weave stories that influence. He will help you create an excellent hypnosis experience for your client. Bob is an expert on Aesop's Fables and often you will feel he is actually Aesop, channeling his wit and wisdom. Aesop told his stories to the Kings and Queens and Bob tells his story now, for your change work. He offers great techniques however, you must be patient, the magic of stories will unfold as you read. My favorite is the Hare and the Tortoise. I learned a skill many years ago and it is still my philosophy today, "Do it slow, do it right, do it fast, do it twice!" If you are new to the profession of hypnosis or have been doing it over 50 years as I have you will come out of this book with a wisdom yes, a wisdom not just an education you had not been aware of prior. I commend Bob Martel for bringing light to me as he has. Bob concludes his marvelous book on telling stories, by reminding us we can all tell a story. Read Bob's book from cover to cover and stories will be easy for you to tell your clients. He makes it easy for you to learn to tell hypnotic stories to your clients. Just pretend you are telling a child a story. And aren't most of your client's children once they are hypnotized waiting with anticipation for your next word. I waited often in this wonderful read, like a child anticipating Bob's next word. He has created true magic. This is a Hypnosis book that, to this point, has never been written. It is a first!"

- Larry Garrett,
Master Hypnotist and author of Healing the Enemy.

Why Read This Book

I am sure you have enjoyed an occasional story someone shared. You were spellbound and mesmerized and at some point, that story resonated with you. You found the value, assigned the meaning, and subconsciously stored it for future reference.

Looking back down the timeline of Aesopic writing, back to 600 BC or so, I wonder if you can imagine, given the worldwide popularity of Aesop's Fables amongst children and adults, just how many fabulists have preceded you. I wonder today, based on my research in writing this book, just how many Aesopian fabulists are penning new fables for us to enjoy and interpret for our own purposes.

Aesop is popular for a reason. For those, like you, willing to explore his works and the impact of a good fable on the direction of one's life, it becomes crystal clear. Quite simply, my hope for you is that you will discover now, as an adult, or perhaps rediscover the magic of Aesop's Fables which should be familiar from childhood and early school days. My hope, also, is that it ignites a spark that rekindles your enthusiasm for storytelling as a powerful tool in clinical hypnosis work or, it lights a fire within you for the first time perhaps, excited about the role of a good story, told in the form of a fable, in your clinical work or as a caregiver or teacher.

Oh, and you should read this book to feed your imaginative mind and have a little fun in the process. Whether you simply read for curiosity or to hone your own storytelling craft, I'm confident you will discover on this quest that you do, indeed, have a vivid imagination – as if channeling Aesop himself.

In the larger picture, I want you to learn how to apply and modify the morals of Aesop's Fables to client situations and ultimately create your own fables. All good reasons to turn the page and keep reading; all toward you in your quest of becoming a better professional hypnotist and, for parents, teachers and all others; to be a more influential counsel, even if just to yourself!

Read this book to further hone skills or to begin your journey as a craftsman of the ancient art of oral storytelling!

The Author's Challenge

Something is compelling you to read this book now. That's great!

Decide to take action and apply the Magic of Aesop!

For professional hypnotists, as you explore the use of Aesop's Fables in your clinical or teaching practice, consider making a commitment to yourself that you will start to add Aesopic storytelling to your change work within the next 30 days.

Table of Contents

Foreword 1

Introduction 5

Chapter One: Getting Started - The Legend of Aesop 14

Chapter Two: Aesopica - Let's Get to Know Aesop a Little Better 45

Chapter Three: Walking A Welcoming Path Forward................... 72

Chapter Four: Feelings. Nothing but Feelings ... and Desires!..... 87

Chapter Five: Meet Aesop, Phaedrus and Babrius (And A Few Other Ancient and Modern Fabulists) 103

Chapter Six: How a Slow and Steady Turtle Changed the World.. 123

Chapter Seven: Thar She Blows? Or Does She?........................ 132

Chapter Eight: To Thine Own Self Be True! 142

Chapter Nine: Four Personal Favorites That Belong in Your Fabulist's Toolbox... 148

Chapter Ten: Aesop, The Servant Leader Storyteller 151

Chapter Eleven: Final Words – Aesop Lives! 157

Appendix A – Resources Consulted 161

Appendix B – Fables and Morals 163

About the Author.. 171

Foreword

Stories are fundamental to human experience. Existing in a world where we have no fur to keep us warm, no claws and only paltry teeth to fight off attackers, and slow reflexes compared to other predators—indeed no physical advantages as a species other than a knack for endurance-running that lies atrophied beyond use in so many of us—knowledge, community, and the ability to share both are traits at the core of our survival. You could argue that being able to use fire and make tools are just as vital, but the knowledge to do both was passed from human to human; often as they gathered around a fire to tell each other stories, creating the first communities.

We don't know the name of the first human to harness fire, but their knowledge has outlived their name. We don't know who wrote Gilgamesh, the first epic poem, but the story they composed is still told and retold, speaking to the futility of mortality as much to us today as it did in ancient Mesopotamia. While a name may be the label of an identity, the story that is told about the identity is the essence of the identity itself.

Who are you? You are a story you tell yourself; your name is just the title of the work. What is your family identity? It is the stories your parents told you about their parents and their grandparents. What is your racial identity? It is the story members of your race and others tell about your genetic group. What is your national identity? It is the story that your nation tells its citizens, and that they tell each other.

Given that story is central to identity, and all of our behavior flows from our identity, the power of changing your story to change your life becomes evident, and indeed the book you are holding is about how a certain set of stories have been transmitting wisdom and changing lives for roughly 2,500 years.

In the profession I share with the author, we call it 'hypnotic storytelling'—but we could just as well call it powerful public speaking, good teaching, effective persuasion, or casting a spell on someone (for what is a spell but a series of words spoken to change reality?)

As hypnotic storytellers, we are collectors of stories. Many of us have spent our whole lives gathering and learning from the wisdom of fables, parables, folktales, moving novels, brilliant short stories, and powerful epics—living vicarious adventures but learning real lessons. For that reason, hypnotic storytellers all have our favorites, and a favorite for many is the fables of Aesop.

Besides being short, easy to remember and retell, cleverly pithy, and overt in their didactic message, Aesop's Fables have the advantage of ubiquity for the hypnotic storyteller. We need barely begin telling one before our clients nod with familiarity. They may not remember the name of the parent, friend, teacher, book, or cartoon that told them that story decades earlier, but they remember the story, because the simple wisdom of Aesop has become embedded in our culture.

Who amongst us, toiling at a seemingly never-ending task, has not recalled the tireless tortoise and muttered, "Slow and steady wins the race"? Who has not felt the tension between the Dog and the Wolf within us, one seeking comfort and the other freedom? Who has not, like the hapless frog drowning in the river, felt the sting of learning that the person we trusted was a scorpion after all? Who has not motivated themselves out of a malaise by recalling, like the carter praying to Hercules for aid, that God helps those who help themselves?

These stories allow us to laugh at ourselves and our problems, making them more manageable—this is a great gift we can give our clients.

And yet, despite the instant rapport generated by reminding a client of a long-forgotten bedtime story, it's a mistake to think that a client must already know one of Aesop's Fables in order for it to resonate. The minute a storyteller begins one, the child within perks up, eager to learn. For that reason, this book is valuable not just to hypnotists, or even just to therapists, but to anyone who seeks to influence or instruct using words: ministers, parents, salesmen, teachers, politicians, leaders … There is a reason that Aesop was honored in his day and is still honored today.

I first met Bob Martel at a hypnosis conference, and we quickly fell to sharing stories. His passion for and knowledge of Aesop impressed me, for I must admit that though I knew a few of the fables, I knew very little about their author, and I had not thoroughly explored the hypnotic applications of the Aesopica.

Soon, you will know more than I did then, and you will be led into this mythical world of talking beasts, hapless humans, and whimsical gods, each living out a metaphor for your edification, by the kindest and gentlest of guides.

You may learn, as I did, that many of the stories attributed to the clever freedman may not have been composed by him, or indeed that Aesop may not have been a real person at all, but simply a name given to a body of work, a label for a collection of timeless wisdom.

In either case, it does not matter. Long after our names and labels have faded; long after the names Elman, Erickson, and Martel are forgotten; their stories will remain.

- James Hazlerig, August 2020

Introduction

Imagine you – an Aesopian storyteller!

You, a fabulous fabulist … just like Aesop! A seemingly extemporaneous inventor of impromptu stories with a moral, designed to influence the mind of your client as you work with them for change. Imagine that! You, a teller of tall tales with a life-changing message for the ears of the recipients.

Yeah, you. Student of the 'sage among sages', as the philosophers of Aesop's time called him.

For the past twelve years, as a professional hypnotist, I have helped clients discover the wisdom of Aesop's Fables to help them make progress in their lives. I have learned how to help my clients achieve unbelievable breakthroughs using the magic of a fable and make unexpected headway toward the shift they are seeking. From developing greater levels of confidence and self-esteem, to overcoming obstacles and facing the challenges in their life, I have used hypnotic stories, especially Aesop's fables, all ready to go with a moral for the mind to embrace. I have learned to use the fable to transport them to a place where they can accept the right hypnotic suggestions to ease their shift to that 'new you' within.

Now, I would like to teach you how to do the same.

Thank you, dear reader, for opening this book. Whether it was a gift, a personal purchase, or provided to you as workshop materials I hope that it will, indeed, make a difference in your life, and that the Magic of Aesop touches others as well.

The formula is easy to follow; read this book with an openness of mind and heart, be present with the stories you read and tell, and remember that you must, in the words of Milton H. Erickson, trust your unconscious mind. It will access your inner resources to make the proper connection to the fables that resonate. In the words of Jerome Bruner in *The Culture of Education,* where he says, "being able to go beyond the information given to 'figure things out' is one of the few untarnished joys of life." He is hinting at the awesome power of our own imagination, something the fable unlocks quite effortlessly. In my mind, every professional hypnotist is a teacher and consultative resource to help a client to learn, explore and discover the world around them as it relates to their presenting issues (and those yet to be revealed in some cases). So, I suggest that you delve into Bruner's work in the field of educational and psychological theory.

No single book will ever do justice to the legend of Aesop and his impact on the world. To this day, his legendary work is studied, dissected, debated and reexamined. Breathe in a sigh of relief for that is not the purpose of this book. It is through sharing a few of Aesop's Fables and explaining how I have used them over the years to assist clients in their journey forward. In fact, I will go so far as to say that *if you read this book* you will certainly enjoy your journey toward improved self-understanding, reminded of or introduced for the first time to Aesop, as you will be getting to know yourself better. In the process of your inner journey work, as you read, you'll be preparing yourself to use the magic of Aesop to accelerate your client's progress toward their own goals.

> *More importantly, said another way, you will improve the effectiveness of your change work with clients as well as cement their lasting success and ease their journey toward the results. For those clients yet to be exposed to the magic of Aesop's Fables, you will be helping them mold their very characters, change perspectives, and examine their self-limiting beliefs. Yes, a solid grasp of his stories (as well as a foundational history into the legend himself) will go a long way toward you becoming a truly masterful agent of change!*

That's my promise to you. I hope my writing about Aesop and sharing my clinical success leads you to this place, a place where you are comfortable 'speaking Aesopian' with your clients. A place where you are comfortable applying the morals of Aesop's Fables to help your clients change a habit, lower their stress and anxiety, improve their performance in daily living and, if it's their goal, to rapidly transform their life. It's all possible by adding the wisdom of a poor, mute, ugly, abused and ridiculed slave named Aesop who lived in Greece 600 years BC, whose legend lives now.

* * * * * *

I confess.

I love fables from all cultures, especially short well-crafted concise stories designed to reach the subconscious mind with a powerful suggestion, either for present moment usage, or for expanded wisdom to be used later in life.

I am absolutely fascinated by Aesop, his fables, and all things 'Aesopica' but this was not always so. He is a legendary figure who mastered the telling of fables to get what he wanted. That was his point! Create influence via a spellbinding story. He was quick-witted; thus, his stories were a bit witty, of course, and somewhat vicious, with an ending that shared wisdom. Magical.

Did your parents read to you as a child?

In thinking about this whole writing project, the inspiration for this book really came from two places I can identify, and it certainly *did not* come from my upbringing. My parents never read stories to us growing up, so it did not come from them. They worked hard raising us. I know their parents could hardly read or write at all. I do know that stories were passed down in past generations. Theoretically, each generation helps the next generation to grow and excel beyond themselves, and stories are integral.

The first source of inspiration was love of a good short story and finding the meaning or lesson within. Secondarily, but of no lesser importance, I started noticing the seemingly magical results I was helping my hypnosis clients to achieve, by either reading directly from Aesop's Fables, sharing a summary, mentioning a moral from a fable as a hypnotic suggestion, or gifting an illustrated copy of Aesop's Fables to a client as part of their program. Clients were having major breakthroughs in the shift they sought for themselves. I simply emphasized that their subconscious mind would hear all that it needed to hear for success today. Since first helping one client end her sugar addition (in the form of twelve cans of Coca cola each day, I've enlisted the wisdom of Aesop to help people stop some very bad habits, to see life through an alternate lens, find the confidence within, to start loving themselves better with more compassion and respect, and to find the courage within to move toward living hypnotically as their more authentic self.

With that said, looking back, I suppose I have always enjoyed listening to a good story, so it was quite natural for me to embrace the notion of storytelling with my clients in my hypnosis practice. I have always admired the eloquence and grace of a true word-master. Yet, more importantly, I was fascinated by a well-structured short story that could penetrate resistance and get a powerful message through to the listener. As you continue reading, you will see new ways of helping people take back more control over the directions of their lives, helping them assess and adjust as they walk the path toward greater happiness.

I need to caution you about my writing style and the sometimes-tangential information that I share. It's a habit, but one that takes me on fabulous journeys as I explore topics on a deep level. When I find a topic I enjoy, I research it. Whether it is my passion for history that drives me or simply a thirst for knowledge that inspires even further understanding, I often absorb myself in the topic. I do hope this book inspires further exploration of Aesop, the man. I'll pull the curtain back a little, as needed, for any foundational understanding. Context is important, as you already know, in a clinical setting. True for storytelling as well.

Journey briefly into your own future. I want you to see yourself as, and then become, a fabulous fabulist just like Aesop. Sharing and expanding fables of the ages and, ultimately, spinning your own, all toward helping the listener or reader to connect with the moral of the story on some level. (Trust me, with my love for a good story, if I can tell his fables or create my own, you can as well.)

Trust the process. Be open. Be mindfully aware, daily, of what is going on in front of you. Let the fable emerge. It will. And you will begin to tell and hear better stories!

Here is a fable I wrote extemporaneously, on the Facebook feed of Michael Hathaway, whom I would call a very mindful hypnotist:

> His post: Some trees grow tall and flexible while others such as fruit trees have the ability to bend when bearing weight. People grow the same way.

> My instant fable: A hypnotist was walking mindfully through the hills of New Hampshire when an acorn dropped from a squirrel high up in an oak tree ... right on the fellow's head. While he pondered whether that was a message from above, he stopped to notice a pear tree, laden with a bountiful yield ... but the mighty oak tree was blocking the sun. And the inflexible and majestic tall oak tree told the pear tree "well, if you don't like it, move. I was here first." The pear tree sent the farmer to the barn to get the chainsaw. Upon seeing this, the oak tree shook and shook, and all his leaves fell to the ground, allowing the sun to shine through and ripen the fruit.

> Moral: (I'll let you decide the lesson from this fable.)

Before you turn the page to begin reading further, whether you have ever read Aesop's Fables to your children, were read to as a child yourself, or simply recall enjoying the magic of hearing a special story read to you at any point in your life, remember that a fable always presents a life-lesson to be embraced and perhaps applied. Yes, this is the magic of stories passed down in every culture; to teach the sage advice and wisdom of our ancestors and those from all walks of life who lived before us.

This book is intended to bring attention to this famous storyteller, Aesop, with the hope that you will discover within you a newfound deeper appreciation for his numerous fables and the lessons designed within. The speaker of truth to power, Aesop's Fables have an important place in clinical hypnosis – delivering good suggestions.

I encourage you to embrace his fables as a tool for self-hypnotic work, and for guiding your clients and loved ones toward the progress they seek. Although this book focuses on the teachings of the secular, Aesop, realized, too, that Jesus was a master storyteller and hypnotist, using parables and his actions to teach values to mankind.

The characters within Aesop's Fables, not surprisingly, are animals who act and talk just like people whilst retaining their animal traits. This theme is especially appealing to children. Animals and nature play a very influential role even today, in commercials that are designed to hypnotize and disarm any resistance to the compliance message being aimed at you.

There are hundreds and hundreds of fables. As you explore the works of Aesop, you'll discover that the fables have been indexed by several people over the centuries. The most famous is from the works of Ben Edwin Perry. His celebrated work, *Aesopica: A Series of Texts Relating to Aesop or Ascribed to Him,* is the most complete collection of the proverbs and fables of Aesop ever assembled. Ben Edwin Perry's exhaustive work remains the definitive edition of all fables reputed to be by Aesop. You may discover any of several indexes of Aesop's Fables, including these:

- Perry Index
- Chambry Index
- Jacobs Index
- Caxton Index

L'Estrange Index

We will primarily consult the Perry Index for this book (when we need to do so, if at all.)

What you should expect from this book

This book will introduce you to Aesop's Fables on a level that you may not yet anticipate. It certainly has led me on an unexpected journey, for in the writing I have honed my fable-telling skills. The fables provide a powerful and easy-to-use tool for change work with hypnosis clients. Often thought to be for children only, they should not be dismissed as such.

As a result of reading, you will be able to:

- Develop a new appreciation for Aesop and his famous fables with the goal of learning how and when to apply his hypnotic stories to client change work in a clinical setting.
- Learn how to map popular fables and 'the moral of the story' to specific client situations in order to accelerate their progress toward success.
- Understand key elements in writing effective 'scripts' that incorporate Aesop's simple methods into a story the client will embrace.
- Create a framework for using Aesop's fables, as a launch point for incorporation of other stories of our time, or passed down orally from long ago, to tap into the imagination of clients.
- Create your own fabulous fables, using the world around you.

I hope you enjoy the book, my friend, and that you find therapeutic magic in the selected Aesop's Fables and, as a professional hypnotist, you help your clients to create truly magical and accelerated lasting results. If you are a hypnotist, licensed counselor, nurse, minister, teacher, salesperson, or consultant, you already tell stories to get the attention and compliance of others. That is what this book is all about, and how you can embellish or customize the story to suit your needs and make your point. If you are a parent, this book should help you refine the stories you use to help you teach values to your children.

By the way, if Aesop were alive today, you'd likely be subscribed to his YouTube channel, on his mailing list, downloading new fables from his website, in his social media groups, and attending his presentations at the world's top hypnosis convention.

Now, open your mind, suspend all disbelief and judgement, allow your creative mind to step forward and come with me. Let's go now and journey together to find that fabulous fabulist within. No prior experience required.

> *"I have not purchased a slave. I have purchased a teacher."*
> - Xanthus' Epiphany

In the end, Aesop was too witty for Xanthus to handle and he ultimately gave Aesop his freedom. As you will discover Aesop was, indeed, the teacher's teacher.

So, I invite you, as a teacher and as a student of Aesop, whether a hypnosis practitioner, mental health professional, a parent, a business leader, or a hypnotherapy client to step into the realm of Aesop's Fables and to delve into the magic of Aesop! Stay with me. We start with a couple of chapters about Aesop because it is an important backdrop. Enjoy!

Chapter One:
Getting Started - The Legend of Aesop

*"Among all the different ways of giving counsel I think
the finest and that which pleases the most universally
is fable, in whatever shape it appears."*
- Joseph Addison, 18th Century Poet, Essayist

Giving good counsel. Isn't that what this is all about?

Well, of course. That's the point of this book! I would add that giving good counsel in the form of suggestions and posthypnotic suggestions, through the masterfully told and well-proven fables, brings the conscious and subconscious mind into the story. After all, it has been done for centuries and now it's *your* turn. And, to go a step further, it's about introducing self-counsel to the clients you serve as the morals and lessons of Aesop's Fables are embraced and become suggestions for the subconscious mind, to apply in the moment or even years later!

The magic of the fable happens in the mind of the listener, who will interpret as necessary and utilize as the subconscious enables. Most people can recall many of the words of wisdom passed down in children's stories or simply told to us by authority figures. Many of the very moral values that shape our lives found in tales from ancient Greece, attribute to the legendary Aesop.

You might recall this sampling:

The Hare and the Tortoise: Never give up! (Hmmm … that was Churchill's motto as well.)

- The Ant and the Grasshopper: Work hard and play hard.
- The Crow and the Pitcher: There is always a way! Necessity is the mother of invention.
- The Two Crabs: Lead by example!
- The Ant and the Dove: One good turn deserves another!
- The Lion and the Mouse: No act of kindness is ever wasted!
- The North Wind and the Sun: Kindness wins people over!
- The Lion, the Ass, and the Fox: Learn from the failures of others!
- Hercules and the Waggoner: The gods help them that help themselves!
- The Wolf and the Crane: Do not always expect a reward in return!

There are, of course, myriad fables to explore, but not here. I've selected a handful of favorites that I use in the office (and share with my grandchildren). We will discuss a handful of fables in this book, in the context of clinical hypnosis work and helping clients transform their lives or make a series of small changes. You'll find that as you utilize fables in your trance work, clients realize that they have the answers within and, as psychologist Jerome Bruner surmised (in my words), it is the journey of self-education that is so enlightening. It brings a certain discovery of increased self-control and inner peace when one uses their own mind to solve things.

Once Upon A Time

In the beginning, at the time of Aesop, it was considered quite highbrow by the elites of that era to 'know your Aesop', which was a challenge because his stories were all shared through oral tradition. Philosophers revered in all things Aesopian. Way back in that time, fabulists were finding all sorts of new and exciting stories to share, as well as sharing the magic of Aesop throughout Greece and Turkey.

Aesop was quick-witted. He had to be in order to survive and in the end his creative fable failed to prevent the citizens of Delphi from throwing him off a cliff, where he met an untimely death. Stories about Aesop using fables to influence and get a point across are found in *The Life of Aesop* (in Greek), with some hints of such stories in various other literature. Perhaps the best chronology of the stories can be found in Laura Gibbs' Aesop's Fables by Oxford University Press.

Aesop: The Wise Fool ... Creator of Mind Magic

Mind magic: the access and utilization of one's own full mind, conscious and subconscious; that seemingly mysterious but ever-present power source that exists to protect and serve our mind, body and spirit. (Author's definition)

Consider this, from what scholars call The Life. While under the servitude of his first master Demarchus, Aesop is well-known for this fable:

> *Æsop going on a journey for his master, along with other slaves of the household, and there being many burdens to*

16

carry, he begged they would not overload him. Looking upon him as weak in body, his fellow-slaves gave him his choice of a load. On this, Æsop selected the pannier of bread, which was the heaviest burden of all, at which his companions were amazed, and thought him a fool. Noon came, however, and when they had each partaken of its contents, Æsop's burden was lightened by one half. At the next meal all the bread was cleared out, leaving Æsop with only the empty basket to carry. At this their eyes were opened, and instead of the fool they at first thought him, he was seen to be the wisest of them all.

A fool, Aesop was not, as this fable he shared:

A mean fellow, seeing Æsop in the street, threw a stone at him. 'Well done!' was his response to the unmannerly action. 'See! here is a penny for you; on my faith it is all I have, but I will tell you how you may get something more. See, yonder comes a rich and influential man. Throw a stone at him in the same way, and you will receive a due reward.' The rude fool, being persuaded, did as he was advised. His daring impudence, however, brought him a requital he did not hope for, though it was what he deserved, for, being seized, he paid the penalty.

As George Fyler Townsend states in his 1874 translation, *Aesop's Fables,* "one of the privileges of a freedman in the ancient republics of Greece, was the permission to take an active interest in public affairs; Aesop, like the philosophers Phaedo, Menippus, and Epictetus, in later times, raised himself from the indignity of a servile condition, to a position of high renown. In his desire alike to instruct and to be instructed, he travelled through many countries, and among others came to Sardis, the capital of the famous king of Lydia, the great patron, in that day, of learning and of learned men.

17

He met at the court of Croesus with Solon, Thales, and other sages, and is related so to have pleased his royal master, by the part he took in the conversations held with these philosophers, that he applied to him an expression which has since passed into proverb, 'The Phrygian has spoked better than all.'" Society began to respect and appreciate Aesop as a witty freedman, worthy of their attention.

Aesop's fables were first captured in written form in Greek and translated to Latin. Phaedrus wrote in Latin, about 250 years before Christ. Babrius wrote in Greek, about 200 years after Christ. As other now-famous fabulists modified and created new fables in both languages, each translation brought about new modifications. Maximus Planudes wrote *The Life of Aesop,* which has been translated. Isaac Nevelet wrote his collection of 286 fables in 1610 in his collection *Mythologica Aesopica*. William Caxton, writer and translator introduced the first printing press to England (and England's first retailer of printed books) and published Caxton's Aesop in Westminster in 1784. Aesop's Fables became a clearly natural choice for book publishing as printing was getting its start. In fact, *The Subtyl Historyes and Fables of Esope*, translated from the French, was one of the books printed by Caxton at his press in Westminster Abbey. Caxon was followed by France's most famous fabulist, Jean de La Fontaine who published 239 fables over 26 years from 1668 to 1694.

All of this, of course, laying the groundwork and fueling the frenzy of Aesop's Fables in England. Why the quote from Joseph Addison at the top of the chapter? He was believed to be the one who started or fed the English fascination (and the beginning of the shift to Aesop's Fables being primarily for children, as they were used in schoolbooks to teach the English language.)

"In Fable, all Things hold discourse; The Words, no doubt, must talk, of course."

Ay and No: A Fable - Works of Jonathan Swift (1726, p 782)

Joseph Addison influenced several Augustan writers of the day. Fables had made their way into early 18th century England. 1697 brought the fables from Paris to London and in 1711, Addison's Mr. Spectator magazine essentially cemented the fable into English culture across a wide spectrum. The fables were and still are quite magical. As Professor Jayne Lewis says in her book, *The English Fable,* "Hence the poets John Dryden, Anne Finch, and John Gay each used Aesopian methods to comment on politics of representation. As fabulists they used their talents to stir debate. These Augustan writers defined a fable as a story that could, if you looked for it, a double meaning but not always. Wit and cunning contributed to the lesson to be found within."

The magic of Aesop's Fables is the power to capture attention, transcend resistance with such a compelling and obvious truth, told through fictional stories on the lips of animals and objects, all designed to get one's point across and get one's way. That is probably why fables are so popular–they work! And it is time to put them to work in your clinical hypnosis practice!

And fables are an entertaining way to connect with people as you share your hypnotic stories. More importantly, in the context of clinical hypnosis, fables are about helping people achieve a breakthrough in their lives by applying the wisdom of Aesop's Fables.

Now, just imagine lowering a listener's internal resistance simply by hearing you tell a good story that resonates with their subconscious mind, connecting on a profound level, all driven by their own intentions, goals, dreams and desires for change. All designed to connect and make progress together, influencing direction and the choices one makes in life, for their betterment.

Well, thanks to all the hard work of a famous storyteller once unable to speak but given that gift by the gods, it is all done for you. His sage advice has been handed down, transcribed, expanded, contracted, and frequently rewritten for the times, all ready for you to use as they are, or with customization to your client's needs. More on that later.

Now, let me ask you. Are you ready to be transported to that magical place within your mind where all things are within reach? A place where the impossible seems so achievable? A place where obstacles that once held you back simply disappear, allowing you to move forward?

As you read to understand and to select appropriate stories for your clients, prepare yourself to enjoy a journey to a place of discovery and greater awareness. Truthfully, it may be better at times to all your clients' unconscious minds to select the best fable for their purposes. As you explore, you will learn more about yourself as you experience the fables I have selected. Take yourself to a place where your child-like curiosity leads you on an adventure that, well, simply never ends, creating a newfound or enhanced resource for connecting with people and making a difference in their lives (as well as your own). You see, the morals of the fables presented in this book, as well as those of Aesop's entire portfolio, should resonate within yourself as an ethical practitioner, and will become tools for you in crafting meaningful suggestions for your clients. Their subconscious mind will easily embrace the lessons. Of course, whether they apply them is entirely their choice.

I am sure you will find, as you immerse yourself in Aesopica, beyond what you learn in this book.

"Aesop's Fables" (Lat: *"Aesopica"*) refers to a collection of well-known fables credited to Aesop, a slave and storyteller who lived in

ancient Greece in the 6th Century BCE. It is also sometimes used as a blanket term for any collections of short fables (i.e. any brief story used to illustrate a moral lesson), especially beast fables involving anthropomorphic animals. They have been popular throughout history and remain a popular choice for morals even today.

It's important to note that over the centuries, Aesop's Fables have evolved to fit the times, most likely starting with the poet Phaedrus, who set the fables to prose, based on oral versions and adding his own style. It's also said that Aesop's works are the second most popularly read stories in literature, only outpaced by the Bible. Several centuries after Phaedrus, others translated and modified Aesop's Fables to suit the author's style and influenced by the times. Maxiumus Planudes, a Byzantine Greek scholar, penned *The Life of Aesop* in fifteenth century Constantinople. His work is considered the first written story about Aesop.

Aesop's Fables are certainly universal; an archetype that has been imitated throughout history, and they have enjoyed the inclusion in the storytelling tradition across world cultures. His fables have:

- Influenced the Gospel of Mark.
- Been found in the Koran (Aesop is called Luqman).
- Referenced by the Sufi mystical poet, Jalaluddin Rumi.
- Been featured in dramatizations and plays.
- Been set to musical scores.
- Permeated political discourse in jolly old England and elsewhere.
- Provided life lessons for children and adults around the globe.

And now Aesop is coming to a clinical hypnosis office near you!

Robert Martel

All Good Stories are Hypnotic – Thus the Popularity and Magical Effect of Aesop

It is no wonder that Aesop is so popular!

Fables are indeed hypnotic. Hypnotic storytelling is well recognized as an effective tool in our profession and throughout society across all cultures. I grant you that storytelling may seem a bit intimidating to many hypnotists and counselors.

This book should teach you confidence in creating a fable-sharing framework that you can use in your practice, meaning you should be able to construct a map of sorts to choose the best fable to fit the circumstance. Start with the fables showcased in this book and then choose one that allows even the timidest hypnotist to success with this method. Aesop wrote more than 150 fables, which have been handed down and translated for the modern era and are still used today to teach valuable lessons and gain important insights to life. A good story, one that captures the imagination, is always hypnotic. Whether in a clinical setting, by the campfire, or simply with family and friends. The words, the delivery, the timeliness of the message within, if any, all combine to stir the emotions especially if this story contains a lesson or moral. A well-told and well-structured story has the power to lower resistance and to help open one's mind to new possibilities, new ways of thinking.

For as long as I have been using hypnosis as a tool for influencing and accelerating transformational change, I have always relied upon a good story, either extemporaneously constructed on the spot, or handed down from the ages to help clients see things from a new point of view. I should add that I've always been somewhat of a storyteller of sorts, something I discovered in my youth, in the US Navy, in raising my three sons, and throughout my professional life.

The inspiration for this book, the spark, comes from change work in my hypnotherapy practice. As I have stated earlier, I use storytelling with just about every client, mostly from Aesop and I've learned to create stories on the spot or for a subsequent client session.

True story.

Once upon a time, I had a particularly challenging client who was (supposedly) open and receptive to changing her limiting habits, perhaps fearing the change a bit, and one whose progress was becoming elusive. She was stuck, could not determine the cause, and was losing confidence and hope in her ability to make the progress she sought. Aesop to the rescue! I actually gifted her a copy of an illustrated Aesop's Fables and asked her to trust our process of subconscious communication and, in reading the fables, her mind would find meaning to her situation.

I offer this book to introduce a building block to the professional hypnotist, toward introducing or refining the tool of hypnotic storytelling and to help illustrate just how easy it is to add stories to your change work, even if you struggle to construct a story yourself. My client was getting discouraged. On her way out of my office, being fully aware of the child within each of us, throughout life, I handed her a children's book, Aesop's Fables, which I routinely hand out to select clients as part of their program when it was appropriate to share. With the assignment to read the fables to her child and to reflect on her efforts to change with the aid of hypnotherapy, she returned having resolved her issues, and fully ready to accept suggestions for her highest and best. I calculated, and rightly so, that my hypnosis clients would enjoy a good story, woven into the fabric of their mind.

While it is so tempting to begin this book with 'once upon a time', I will refrain from doing so. Too cliché, although it is a hypnotic phrase that triggers the attention of the imaginative mind. Your new fable-telling skills will easily attract the attention of your listeners. Well told, a good story captures our imagination before the storyteller begins, and once started it allows our mind to take whatever lessons it extracts and applies them as necessary, throughout life's journey, to help us make good healthy decisions for ourselves.

The right metaphors and similes combined with the right strings of words compel us to listen, almost if not fully, in a hypnotic state, allowing the magic of the story to become a part of us. When we can relax ourselves, even treat ourselves to enjoy a good story, we feed our mind – our wonderfully mysterious and magical mind – with the information or perspective that we need in order to see things as they are now or should become as the future unfolds.

A Tale, A Parable and A Fable

A fable is best defined as a fiction picturing a truth, either a point or a moral. There were numerous famous fabulists of Aesop's era and in years hence. Many tried to emulate him, many have been credited with some of Aesop's fables, and still others have been credited for storying that were his. In the world of Aesopica, scholars all agree that the picture is murky. Some wonder whether if he ever lived. Babrius is known for several fables. Phaedrus has many fables attributed to his name, as do Avianus, Abstemius and many others whose collections may be found in the 1921 book, *An Argosy of Fables: A Representative Selection from the Fable Literature of Every Land and Culture, and in the equally important book, The Talking Beasts: A book of Fable Wisdom,* which presents fables from across world cultures.

What is unique about the fable? Quite simply, it is short, mesmerizing and delivers a thought-provoking moral for our own

24

values system to consider and embrace. But let us not reinvent the wheel here. I want to build a foundation and share insights into the structure of a fable so you can differentiate it from other short-form stories with a message.

As George Fyler Townsend shares in his 1884 translation, Aesop's Fables,

"THE TALE, the Parable, and the Fable are all common and popular modes of conveying instruction. Each is distinguished by its own special characteristics. The Tale consists simply in the narration of a story either founded on facts, or created solely by the imagination, and not necessarily associated with the teaching of any moral lesson. The Parable is the designed use of language purposely intended to convey a hidden and secret meaning other than that contained in the words themselves; and which may or may not bear a special reference to the hearer, or reader. The Fable partly agrees with, and partly differs from both of these. It will contain, like the Tale, a short but real narrative; it will seek, like the Parable, to convey a hidden meaning, and that not so much by the use of language, as by the skillful introduction of fictitious characters; and yet unlike to either Tale or Parable, it will ever keep in view, as its high prerogative, and inseparable attribute, the great purpose of instruction, and will necessarily seek to inculcate some moral maxim, social duty, or political truth. The true Fable, if it rise to its high requirements, ever aims at one great end and purpose representation of human motive, and the improvement of human conduct, and yet it so conceals its design under the disguise of fictitious characters, by clothing with speech the animals of the field, the birds of the air, the trees of the wood, or the beasts of the forest, that the reader shall receive advice without perceiving the presence of the adviser. Thus the superiority of the counsellor, which often renders counsel unpalatable, is kept out of view, and the lesson comes with the greater acceptance when the reader is led, unconsciously to himself, to have his sympathies enlisted in behalf of what is pure, honorable, and praiseworthy, and to have his indignation excited against what is low, ignoble, and unworthy. The true fabulist, therefore, discharges a most important function. He is neither a narrator, nor an allegorist. He is a great teacher, a corrector of morals, a censor of vice, and a commander of virtue. In this consists the superiority of the Fable over the Tale or the Parable. The fabulist is to create a laugh, but yet, under a merry guise, to convey instruction. Phaedrus, the great imitator of Aesop, plainly indicates this double purpose to be the true office of the writer of fables."

Just like Phaedrus in his day, in your own creative style, you are moving closer to becoming a better teller of mesmerizing fables. Think about it, because it is happening as you continue to read this book. Yes, imagine you, a fabulous fabulist, a teller and a creator of great fables with great lessons for life. But, let me offer one more definition of a fable, circa 1896, by Thomas Newbigging. Indulge me please.

"The Aesopian fable or apologue is a short story, either fictitious or true, generally fictitious, calculated to convey instruction, advice or reproof, in an interesting form, impressing its lesson on the mind more deeply than a mere didactic piece of counsel or admonition is capable of doing. We say a short story, because if the narration is spun out to a considerable length it ceases to be a true fable in the ordinary acceptation of the term, and becomes a tale, such, for example, as a fairy tale. Now, a fairy or other fanciful tale usually or invariably contains some romance and much improbability; it often deals largely in the superstitious, and it is not necessarily the vehicle for conveying a moral. The very opposite holds good of a fable. Although animals are usually the actors in the fable, there is an air of naturalness in their assumed speech and actions. The story may be either highly imaginative or baldly matter-of-fact, but it never wanders beyond the range of intuitive (as opposed to actual or natural) experience, and it always contains a moral. In a word, a fable is, or ought to be, the very quintessence of common sense and wise counsel couched in brief narrative form. It partakes somewhat of the character of a parable, though it can hardly be described as a parable, because this is more sedate in character, has human beings as its actors, and is usually based on an actual occurrence.

Though parables are not fables in the strict and limited meaning of the term, they bear a close family relationship to them. Parables may be defined as stories in allegorical dress. The Scriptures, both old and new, abound with them. The most beautiful example in the Old Testament is that of Nathan and the ewe lamb, in which David the King is made his own accuser. This was a favourite mode of conveying instruction and reproof employed by our Lord. Christ often 'spake in parables'; and with what feelings of reverential awe must we regard the parables of the Gospels, coming as they did from the lips of our Saviour!"

The Basic Structure of An Aesopian Fable

In his article, *Listening to Aesop's Animals*, Jeremy Lefkowitz, Associate Professor of Classics at Strathmore College (and a passionate Aesopian guru, in my eyes) astutely writes:

> *The legendary Aesop, whom Herodotus places on Samos in the 6th century BCE (Histories, 2.134), did not write a single fable with his own hand. The fables that have survived under his name were written in the centuries after his death, composed by a diverse set of writers who labeled their stories "Aesop's" with little concern for historical accuracy. We are left with hundreds of tales and anecdotes scattered across the remains of Classical literature, in both Greek and Latin, in prose and in verse, each one with murky origins and dubious links to the life of Aesop .... The philosophical*

27

content of Aesop's fables is perhaps best described as "popular" or "applied" ethic. Like other ancient satirical genres (e.g., iambography, Greek comedy, Roman satire), fables describe and condemn common varieties of misbehavior, especially greed, hypocrisy, vanity, and deceit. But two salient features set the fable apart from other forms of moralizing literature: (1) the drawing out of an explicit message in the form of a moral; and (2) the use of talking animals as protagonists .... According to our ancient sources, the fable's use of animals primarily serves to underscore the fictionality and lightness of the stories. The risibility of the humanized animal allows the fable to make its point without boring or insulting an addressee. So, it follows, while calling someone an "ass" might reasonably cause offense, fable-tellers can be more effective and more politic by offering advice or criticism with a made-up story. Take, for example, this excerpt from "The Ass in the Lion's Skin" (Perry, 188):

> An ass put on a lion's skin and went around frightening the other animals (ta aloga zoa). He saw a fox and tried to terrify her, too. But she happened to have heard his voice and said to him, "I can assure you I would have been afraid of you, too, if I hadn't heard your braying." So it is that some ignorant men who create an impression of being someone by their outward elegance expose themselves by their own talkativeness (glōssalgias).

By bringing to the fore the fictitious nature of the story, animal fables entertain and establish that the only possibility of serious meaning is the interpretation; the auditor must listen to the moral and decide if the fable applies.

Now, I share the above, with attribution for his eloquent observation, because he has captured the very argument for using Aesop's fables in the clinical hypnosis setting or in any event where the offering of such nonthreatening stories, as told by talking animals, are deemed appropriate. We merely need to help the client to hear the 'spoken word' of Aesop's animals and then allow their subconscious mind to assign the meaning of the moral found within the story.

But Where is the Moral to the Story?

Scholars have studied the fables *ad infinitum* to appreciate, dissect or imitate the magic of the fable structure. I do not expect you to delve into the myriad scholarly books on the subject. Accept the fact that many argued over the integrity, structure, and purpose of a fable. Include the moral, or leave the lesson to interpretation?

Yet, through the centuries, for the most part, the casual reader of Aesop's fables and the fables of others who followed, can certainly find the lesson within each story. In fact, there are several morals to be gleaned, some overt, some covert, and others influenced by the times in which they are read, and sometimes merely for humorous or political meaning.

As Laura Gibbs states in her book, Aesop's' Fables, A New translation:

> "While there is no hard and fast definition of an Aesop fable, it is the moral of the story that most clearly distinguishes the fable from other kinds of humorous anecdotes or jokes; jokes have punch-lines, fables have morals. Typically, the moral of the story is expressed by one of the characters in the very last words, the same position occupied by the punchline of a

joke. Unlike the punch line, however, a moral conveys a message or lesson."

Let's quickly look at the placement of the morals in a fable. Doing so is like dissecting one of your best clinical hypnosis sessions with a client. Think about a time where you worked with a client and great progress was apparent. Did you plant a seed about telling a story at a future session, or set anticipation for a story that "may just be what the mind needs to hear"?

La Fontaine, France's hero of the fable said in 1668, "The fable proper is composed of two parts, of which one may be termed the *body* and the other the *soul*. The *body* is the subject-matter of the fable and the soul is the moral." Joseph Jacobs argued, "On the origin of the added morals to fables, Mr. Joseph Jacobs has the following appropriate remarks: 'The fable is a species of the allegory, and it seems absurd to give your allegory, and then give in addition the truth which you wish to convey. Either your fable makes its point, or it does not. If it does, you need not repeat your point: if it does not, you need not give your fable. To add your point is practically to confess the fear that your fable has not put it with sufficient force. Yet this is practically what the moral does, which has now become part and parcel of a fable. It was not always so; it does not occur in the ancient classical fables. That it is not an organic part of the fable is shown by the curious fact that so many morals miss the point of the fables."

Pro Tip: My advice, based on Jacobs interpretation of a fable, and Gibb's definition, is that you choose amongst Aesop's Fables those that have a clear moral. In the case where the moral is seemingly more hidden, you may have to guide your client to see it, or simply allow them to arrive at their own meaning, as we know that the reader/listener always assigns the meaning.

Let us agree that, as clinicians, there are times to include and times to exclude the moral, so that 'self-discovery' may take place. The true moral of the story is contained within the fable itself and resonates with the subconscious mind. If you are inclined to write your own fables, as you become a masterful fabulist yourself, you will need to be aware of where within the fable you place the moral!

Here are the three places where you will find a moral, hidden in plain sight, or out in the open:

- The Moral May Be an *Epimythium:* from the Greek epi-mythos (after-story), something that follows the fable, as Gibbs says, "it is added by the teller to make sure the point is absolutely clear". It is the conclusion or lesson, as spoken by one of the (animal) characters. As you will discover, the morals of early fabulists were written, rewritten, and modified through the ages, by various translators, to fit the times.

- It Could Be a *Promythium:* from the Greek pro-mythos (before-story), indicating that it comes before the fable itself. Hey, sometimes you need to tell them what you are going to tell them, before you tell them!

- Or It Could Be an *Endomythium:* from the Greek endo-mythos (inside-story), indicating exactly that! There's always an inside story to the fables you tell, and many times if not most, your clients and perhaps yourself are telling an endomythium, or inside story about your life, your circumstances, emotional state or general level of mental health.

- Or, if omitted from, in the words of the author, the Greek moral-not-present-mythos, (no-story), indicating it is a mystery for the mind to process!

Why is positioning of the moral important to you as a professional hypnotist (or teacher)?

As you select fables based on the client's presenting situation and their goals, you may decide, off the cuff, to slip in a moral as you would a posthypnotic suggestion. For example, at the end of the first session you may even say: *"Bill, that reminds me of a person who decided to go for the low hanging fruit."* Without mentioning Aesop, in the next session you can bring up The Fox and The Grapes. In this example, you planted the moral in his mind – or helped him reconnect to it, and on his way home from the second session or even sooner, he'll begin to extract meaning! Or, reverse that process. On the way out from the first session, you may hand Bill a sheet with that fable (or any other as appropriate) and when he returns the moral gets inserted into your hypnotic suggestions for the second session. You don't have to beat that horse too hard, but that's a fable for another day!

The Magic Formula for Fabulous Fables

Aesop knew it. He mastered it, in fact. So did Homer, 200 years earlier. So did Eve in the Garden of Eden. You'll find the spellbinding magic formula for storytelling in today's modern world and you'll engage groups, friends you meet, and your clients, of course! By the time you finish this book you will be a natural! Yes, far beyond becoming a master at applying fables in your clinical work, you'll be using the structure of a fable to influence and persuade people in all sorts of ways.

Fables are the type of short story whereby, when all is said and done (recognize that moral?), somehow the message bypasses the mind's critical faculty and sinks deep into the subconscious mind, to be called up and applied as circumstances arise. That is the magic, and this no-fail formula will ensure you deliver powerful messages to the subconscious minds of all in earshot of your stories, and those retold Aesop fables.

While this is not a fable writing workshop, there are some special components to each effective hypnotic story in this literary genre we call a fable. Here's 'Martel's formula' for structuring a good hypnotic fable, essentially my observations as a student of the fable and from using fables in the office to spark transformational change:

(Attention x Rapport x Curiosity x Relevance) = meaning + Value + Resonance

Attention	the act or state of applying the mind to something, a condition of readiness for such attention involving especially a selective narrowing or focusing of consciousness and receptivity
Rapport	a friendly, harmonious relationship, especially a relationship characterized by agreement, mutual understanding, or empathy that makes communication possible or easy
Curiosity	desire to know more; inquisitive interest
Relevance	relation to the matter at hand, practical and the ability (as of an information retrieval system) to retrieve material that satisfies the needs of the user

Meaning	the thing one intends to convey especially by language, especially by language, intended
Value	something (such as a principle or quality) intrinsically desirable, relative worth, utility, or importance
Resonance	a quality of evoking response, the quality or state of being resonant, intensified and enriched

Thank you, Merriam-Webster!

Which, of course, having these factors well addressed leads to improved influence and compliance with the message they are engaged and receptive to hear, and the recipient's acceptance of any lessons they may draw (whether it's the moral of the fable as engineered, or something their mind extracted).

In other words, you increase compliance when you master the above formula!

Metaphors Within and Beyond the Fable

In subsequent chapters, you will see how to utilize the fable as it is written and *as it can become,* with your creativity and imagination, and that of the client as well. As you work with your client, listening to their 'script' as they reveal it (usually) in the first session, note their words and language patterns, becoming clues for you in selecting fables and morals for consideration for subsequent sessions.

Pro Tip: Usually, in the second session I will plant the seed toward the end of the time together with a sentence like, *"hey ... that's a fascinating point ... you've reminded me of story I remember as a kid ... but we're almost at the end for today ... in case I forget ... remind me next time we're together to tell you the story.*" Then make a note of the story you intend to share! I will often print the story for their return visit on letterhead, as one of several handouts they receive for at home and post-program work, and I'll leave space for their notetaking. On occasion, if I find the client hitting a wall or feeling hopeless about making progress I will 'gift' them a copy of an illustrated version of popular fables. I always, in this case, precede the gift-giving with a little discussion about their commitment to keep an open, non-judgmental mind and to let their inner child step forward. When I gift them a book I always say, *"who knows how your mind will respond? Your job is simply to enjoy these fables ... get lost in the fable itself, patiently letting the story unfold – as silly as it may seem at first and let the moral reveal itself. I wonder if you will be the kind of person who easily and readily relaxes into the mode of exploring these fabulous stories ... or if you'll take some time for some self-hypnosis work to get into that mind state. In any case, let your mind find the connection. There is no reason to try to find meaning ... meaning will appear magically, effortlessly, and automatically. Just enjoy the journey of discovery .... Enjoy the story itself .... The characters ... the animals and trees ... how they talk ... Can you do that?"*

It's worked for me and many, many clients!

Ah, the Micro-Fable

Sometimes you need to tell a fable under pressure or in the case when time is simply of the essence. In these instances, you will appreciate the micro-version of any fable, which you will customize to the scenario. (Depending on your comfort level in telling fables, the micro-fable, written in your own words as a short summary, may do the trick!)

A micro-fable, in a clinical application, is a great way to deliver a posthypnotic suggestion, even as you say goodbye to the client in the office or if you are ending an online video session. You can choose to include the moral or omit it for discussion and let the client's mind extract the value. Timing is important. Think 'rapport' and trance utilization, and how you can focus the client on the story itself and on storytelling as a therapeutic tool for healing, for progress or what have you. Even something as simple as, *"hey, Bill, stay with me for a moment ... because this is so important to what we're doing together,"* will keep their attention for the micro-fable.

Here is a real example of a micro-fable in action:

> Bound for Las Vegas I boarded a JetBlue flight in Boston. I was seated in the aisle seat. The woman in the middle was travelling with her husband, who had been instructed to lower the shades. She was whimpering, jacket over her head, obviously afraid of flying. I introduced myself and offered to help her, so she'd enjoy her flight to Vegas and vacation time with her hubby. She nodded. So, I said...

> "Okay. The captain just announced it was a busy morning on the tarmac and we were number ten in line, but we'd be in the air quickly, probably three minutes or so. Now, just close your eyes and listen to me ... and ... hey ... do you recall Aesop's Fables? (Yes). Great! All I want you to do is think of your memories about Aesop's fables .... Okay? I do not have time to tell you one ... I want to help you end this now ... so access your favorite story now ... 3, 2, 1 ... I hope you chose the Hare and Tortoise. That silly rabbit ... well, quicker than he can jump around that determined turtle ... I want to say ... (Pilot interrupts to say we are sixth in line for take-off) before I say more ... before the pilot comes on again and says we are third or second or next ... I wonder if

you'll be smiling out the window with your jacket in your lap … fear all gone. Oh … now … I want you to take a deep breath … another … and one more … breathing out all fear because I know you are just as brave, courageous and strong as that determined turtle." Captain announced we were second in line. Shades up. Smile. Coat in lap. Voila. I got an email from her two days later thanking me. She and her husband were already planning their next vacation!

You can do this, too. Chances are you already have done something similar. As we explore Aesop, and you become armed with the proper references to morals and indexes of fables as you see fit, you will learn how to use extemporaneous micro-fables in and out of the clinical setting.

To illustrate by example, here is a micro-fable of the original The Nightingale's Advice, as written by Laura Gibbs in her micro-fables blog, where she tells her own 100-word version of the fable. Following it, you will find a second example of a 'drabble', a 100-word summary of a fable.

The Nightingale's Advice (Perry Index – 627, rewritten as a micro-fable)

A bird-catcher captured a nightingale. "I'll give you three pieces of advice," said the nightingale. "If you like my advice, please set me free." The man agreed. "When you've lost something, let it go. Don't grieve over your loss. And don't believe in the impossible." "Very wise," said the man, releasing her. "You fool!" chirped the bird, flying up in the sky. "There's a ruby in my stomach as big as an ostrich egg." The man bewailed his loss. "You really are a fool!" she said. "Remember the advice I gave you: all of it!" Laughing, the bird flew away.

The Swallow and the Nightingale (Perry Index – 277, rewritten as a micro-fable)

The swallow, flying through the woods, heard the nightingale singing. "Dear nightingale," said the swallow, "your song is so beautiful! Why do you conceal yourself here in the woods? Your song is worthy of a royal audience! Leave this wilderness behind and come with me to where the people live. I will escort you directly to the palace of the king." "No, dear swallow," replied the nightingale, "I don't want to go to the homes of men, nor even to the palaces of kings. I prefer this solitude where I can sing my songs for God and for the angels."

Here's a pro tip! With attribution to Laura Gibbs, if you do use any of her micro-fables at her blog posts, or with your own custom written micro-fable versions of an Aesop original, create a worksheet for clients. If you create one worksheet per week, you will assemble quite a portfolio and you can select the appropriate worksheet for any client situation as homework or a download for use in their self-hypnosis work. I used the two drabbles shown above with a client dealing with a habit of drinking four alcohol nips as sunset was drawing near each evening. I tied the moral of the original fables to his narrative and goals, and we (he) found a connection. He was able to let go of what he thought alcohol was doing for him. Voila!

Learn more about drabbles (tiny traditional stories in 100 words) and micro-fables at Laura Gibb's project: https://microfables.blogspot.com/2020/01/a-guide-to-microfables.html (Note: You'll find some of Laura's great writings on fables from other greats such as Rumi, Panchatantra, Nasruddin and Inayat Khan.)

Keep This in Mind: Aesop's Fables Are NOT Just for Kids (If They Ever Were!)

In fact, they were not written for kids at all. They became children's stories centuries later as they were written and rewritten, passed down through the ages. (In jolly old England, they were rewritten and told to children as a method of teaching the English language, probably common in other cultures. It was William Caxton who, in Westminster Abbey, wrote and printed his version, most likely with children in mind. I am here to tell you that while Aesop is popular with those who teach and read to children, his fables are meant for all, originally told and captured in writing for adults in society. They teach good living, as Jesus, Epictetus, Seneca and Marcus Aurelius also taught.

Aesop's fables were told to and for philosophers of the time, Kings and Queens and, probably most importantly, to Xanthus, his master, for whom the fables helped him maintain his elite standing in life. No, they were not kids' stories at all. Some of them are quite scary!

Whether Aesop actually existed, or if he exists only in our minds, is the subject of another book altogether but a bit more on that later. I lean toward the scholars who have documented his Greek life, and the references to him by Aristotle and Socrates, to name a few. Yes, there is much mystery and legend, intermixed by mythological stories and his historical and documented association with the legend of the Seven Sages of Antiquity, renowned for their wisdom:

> *The Seven Sages (of Greece) or Seven Wise Men (Greek: οι ἑπτὰ σοφοί hoi hepta sophoi) was the title given by classical Greek tradition to seven philosophers, statesmen, and law-givers of the 6th century BC who were renowned for their wisdom. Among these were Thales of Miletus, and Pittacus of Mytilene, and Bias of Priene, and our own Solon, and*

> *Cleobulus of Lindus, and Myson of Chenae, and the seventh of them was said to be Chilon of Sparta.*

So, history has placed Aesop among the wisest of the wise, the storytelling gurus of the 6th century BC. Channel him and bring his wisdom right into your office and the client's transformation.

I once believed, or assumed, that most parents were familiar with Aesop's Fables. After all, Aesop's famous fables and scripts have provided great imaginative experiences and adventures – and teaching opportunities – as I mentioned, now primarily for children and young adults. These short fables or life stories, by their very design, as they have been translated from Greek and Latin, are all very short so keep the attention of children.

But remember this.

You will encounter adult clients who are quick to dismiss the advice of consulting Aesopica to help solve their issue or face a challenge. Selling the idea of reading as adults what are perceived as children's' stories may be an uphill battle and so you'll simply construct a story about the clients who have braved the stigma, blasted through only to access a secret to their success, a missing ingredient that propelled them forward. Or appeal to their child within.

My advice?

Introduce Aesop's Fables in your second or third session with a client. Plant the seeds. You see, in the first session they will admit to keeping an open mind and allowing their subconscious mind to hear suggestions that are beneficial, for their highest and best, without a critical mind. Bingo!

Aesop speaks to the child within each of us by instantly capturing interest in the story.

> Phædrus, in the prologue to his fables, says—
>
> "Tis but a play to form the youth,
>
> By fiction in the cause of truth,"

I think what Phaedrus was saying about Aesop's famed literary genre is that it is in fiction that the mind lets its guard down, suspending disbelief and building trust, allowing the message to be heard. Agree?

The child-like mind within you as with your clients, from early days of life up until the present moment, seeks guidance and wisdom from adults and authority figures, yet stories and, as Aesop proved, stories with a lesson for life, were always popular.

As you explore Aesop here in the selected fables presented in this book, and the numerous stories attributed to him, my further hope is that you become inspired and confident to become a pretty good storyteller yourself. That is the goal!

Storytelling is an art, whether planned for oral delivery, written out for others to enjoy, or extemporaneously shared, remember that fable telling is an art, something that comes from the heart and from the desire to teach, using a magical tool which the subconscious mind seems to embrace very well.

Keep in mind as we proceed, however, that this book is not intended to present a scholarly discussion of his fables or the history thereof. Such analysis, for the true Aesopic aficionado, can be found online via Google or at the Library of Congress site, for starters.

Rather, *this book* is intended to be like a light being shone upon a powerful tool that you may have overlooked or forgotten. May it rekindle your love for the hypnotic storytelling art that every ear enjoys.

So, to wrap up our work to this point, I have channeled Mr. Thomas Newbigging, Scottish historian and the author of *Fables and Fabulists: Ancient and Modern*, published in London, 1896.

> "The ineradicable impression which certain fables have made upon the mind through uncounted generations by their self-evident appropriateness and truth, is well exemplified in *The Wolf and the Lamb; The Fox and the Grapes; The Hare and the Tortoise; The Dog and the Shadow; The Mountain in Labour; The Fox without a Tail; The Satyr and the Man,* who blew hot and cold with the same breath, and others. It is safe to assert that nothing in literature has been more quoted than the fables named. We could not afford to lose them; their absence would be a distinct loss—literature and life would be the poorer without them; and, such being the fact, we are justified in holding those writers in esteem who have contributed to the instruction and entertainment of mankind in the fables they have invented."

I will let the above words of Newbigging shine more light on the magic of fables. Fables are important, as Newbigging states, and now it is your opportunity and challenge to bring (or expand) the art of therapeutic fable-telling to clinical hypnosis.

Chapter Questions:

1. Imagine life in the time of Aesop, in the republics of Greece, 650 years before Christ. Philosophers came from all walks of life to discuss lessons, human values, and the like. Can

you imagine their amazement at the wit and ingenuity of Aesop, who used his fable telling skills to make a point with his master, Xanthus?

2. Think about your own memories of Aesop's Fables that come to mind. Do you have a favorite story? Is there a particular moral of the story that has made a difference in your life? Even if you did not discover the magic of Aesop as a child, are you willing to challenge yourself to master a few fables, perhaps learning to write a few of your own or modify the works of other fabulists?

3. Focus on the change work you do with clients. You, a catalyst, and facilitator for helping a client to see things from a different perspective - with an appreciation for the fable as a tool for change work, even if you do not fully see the application in clinical hypnosis.

4. What draws you to a good short story? Do you have any stories that you currently share with clients, family, or friends? Why do you reconnect with the message? What resonates?

5. Aesop used fables throughout his own daily life, just to survive and to become a freedman. Imagine the quick-witted Aesop, using fables to influence his master to make him a freedman – free to join the philosophers in the 'town square'.

6. Why add fables to your repertoire? How might they fit into your change work? As you may know, or will soon discover, storytelling is very *Ericksonian*. Imagine combining the teachings of Milton H. Erickson with those of Aesop, the Phrygian storyteller.

7. This may be premature to ask. I wonder if you can begin to envision just how you might weave the use of fables into what you already know about a good pre-talk, induction, and overall hypnosis session? How do the rapport-building skills

you already possess and the hypnotic techniques you
continue to master fit in with your planned use of fables?

*Now let us move on to learn more about the legend himself before
we delve into the clinical magic you'll be using in your practice.*

Chapter Two:
Aesopica - Let's Get to Know
Aesop a Little Better

*"Ah, but master, I will bring the food to the one who
loves you most, as instructed. But we will see which
bitch loves you more, your dog or your mistress."*
- Aesop to Xanthus

Aesop was witty but he did not sugarcoat his messages, as the slave became teacher to the slave owner. He often used fables, on the spot, to make a point.

In the age of Aesop and the years following his untimely death at the foot of a seaside cliff in Delphi, keep in mind that the great teachers, philosophers and orators of that era preached the rhetorical value of the fables. If this book sparks you to study Aesop in the classical sense, you will get a very basic grounding here, but you are encouraged to explore the resources found in the appendix.

To start things off, to better understand the age of Aesop, I offer you the following poetic reference to Aesop, likely found in an 1874 book by the un-named English editor known as J.B.R.:

The Power of the Fables of Aesop

'Twas the Golden Age when every brute

Had voice articulate, in speech was skilled,

And the mid-forests with its synods filled.

The tongues of rock and pine-leaf then were free;

To ship and sailor then would speak the sea;

Sparrows with farmers would shrewd talk maintain;

Earth gave all fruits, nor asked for toil again.

Mortals and gods were wont to mix as friends—

To which conclusion all the teaching tends

Of sage old Aesop."

- Babrius (in JBR Preface)

"Don't count your chickens before they are hatched!" "He is a wolf in sheep's clothing." "She has a sour-grapes attitude." "They are killing the goose that laid the golden eggs." "He demands the lion's share." "Don't be like the boy who called 'wolf!'"

These expressions are so much a part of our everyday language and culture that they seem to have been with us forever, and that is almost the case, for the fables that produced these proverbial sayings are indeed even older than (to name but three) the modern English, French, and German languages where today they are so much at home. The fables behind these sayings are those of arguably the most famous storyteller of all time, the legendary Aesop. Who was the man who created these timeless literary gems?

Aesop is justly regarded as the foremost inventor of fables that the world has seen. He flourished, as Thomas Newbigging states in his book, *Aesop's Fables,* in the sixth century before Christ. Several places, as in the case of Homer, are claimed as his birthplace— Sardis in Lydia, Ammorius, the island of Samos, and Mesembra, a city of Thrace; but the weight of authority is in favor of Cotiæum, a city of Phrygia in the Lesser Asia, hence his moniker of 'the Phrygian.'

Straight from Wikipedia, for the streamlined synopsis:

> "Aesop's Fables, or the Aesopica, is a collection of fables credited to Aesop, a slave and storyteller believed to have lived in ancient Greece between 620 and 564 BCE. Of diverse origins, the stories associated with his name have descended to modern times through several sources and continue to be reinterpreted in different verbal registers and in popular as well as artistic media.
>
> The fables originally belonged to the oral tradition and were not collected for some three centuries after Aesop's death. By that time, a variety of other stories, jokes and proverbs were being ascribed to him, although some of that material was from sources earlier than him or came from beyond the Greek cultural sphere. On the arrival of printing, collections of Aesop's fables were among the earliest books in a variety of languages. Through the means of later collections, and translations or adaptations of them, Aesop's reputation as a fabulist was transmitted throughout the world.
>
> Initially the fables were addressed to adults and covered religious, social, and political themes. They were also put to use as ethical guides and from the Renaissance onwards were particularly used for the education of children. Their

ethical dimension was reinforced in the adult world through depiction in sculpture, painting, and other illustrative means, as well as adaptation to drama and song. In addition, there have been reinterpretations of the meaning of fables and changes in emphasis over time."

Let us take a look at these fables, each directly impacting Aesop's life, as documented in several sources but attributed here to Thomas Newbigging and also appearing in various forms in Lloyd Daly's *Aesop Without Morals.*

Those Dastardly Delphinians Killed Aesop!

So Aesop could not convince them through fable, as he attempted. The citizens of Delphi were humiliated by Aesop's superior wit, so over the cliff and into the sea he went. Aye! But Aesop lives, even today, in the hearts and minds of mankind through the ages. Let me share a few stories of Aesopian fables that the legend himself spun:

Xanthus once, when in his cups, had foolishly wagered his land and houses that he would drink the sea dry. Recovering his senses, he besought Æsop his slave to find him a way out of his difficulty. This Æsop engaged to do. At the appointed time, when the foolish feat was to be performed, or his houses and lands forfeited, Xanthus, previously instructed by Æsop, appeared at the seaside before the multitude which had assembled to witness his expected discomfiture. 'I am ready,' cried he, 'to drain the waters of the sea to the last drop; but first of all you must stop the rivers from running into it: to drink these also is not in the contract.' The request was admitted being a reasonable one, and as his opponents were powerless to perform their part, they were covered with derision by the populace, who were loud in their praises of the wisdom of Xanthus.

In other words, Aesop, as he often did in how witty storytelling, called their bluff in that story above, and emerged the victor! He was also master at teaching philosophy to the learned students of Xandrus:

Aesop, a slave to Xanthus on the island of Samos, was ordered one day to arrange the meal for a large banquet. He was to provide the choicest dainties that money could buy. When the guests arrived, they were treated to a starter of tongue, served with a variety of excellent sauces. The guests of course made a few jokes about this. But when the next course was tongue too, they were puzzled. And when the third and fourth courses turned out to be tongue too puzzlement turned to perplexity. Xanthus was embarrassed and turning to Aesop angrily demanded an explanation. 'Didn't I tell you to provide the best meat you could find?' 'What could be better than the tongue?' said Aesop. 'It is the tongue that teaches and enlightens, the tongue that praises and entertains, it is the tongue that strikes bargains and makes promises.' The guests liked what Aesop said and good feeling was restored to the meal. Xanthus spoke up: 'Well, perhaps all of you could do me the favor of coming again for another meal tomorrow?' And turning to Aesop he added, 'This time could you arrange a meal with the worst meat you can find?' The guests liked the idea and returned the following evening. And, to their confusion, nothing but tongue was served again. Xanthus seemed angry. 'How,' he said, 'can you serve up tongue as the best possible meat one day, and then the worst meat the next?' 'What,' replied Aesop, 'can be worse than the tongue? What evil is it not involved in? Violence, injustice and fraud are all debated and resolved upon and communicated by the tongue. It is the ruin of empires, cities and friendships.' The guests were pleased by what Aesop had said and pleaded with Xanthus to appreciate the wisdom of his slave. (This reputation as a wise man eventually earned him his freedom, and thus he embarked on a journey to Delphi.)

For example, from ancient translations:

Aesop was going on a journey for his master, along with other slaves of the household, and there being many burdens to carry, he begged they would not overload him. Looking upon him as weak in body, his fellow-slaves gave him his choice of a load. On this, Æsop selected the pannier of bread, which was the heaviest burden of all, at which his companions were amazed, and thought him a fool. Noon came, however, and when they had each partaken of its contents, Æsop's burden was lightened by one half. At the next meal all the bread was cleared out, leaving Æsop with only the empty basket to carry. At this their eyes were opened, and instead of the fool they at first thought him, he was seen to be the wisest of them all.

A fable to clear his good name!

Aesop did not have it easy.

Trouble always seemed to find him, based on what I glean from research of the early Aesopica translated from Greek and Latin, and retold by numerous translators. Going back to Phaedrus and Babrius, though, you get closer to the original. The morals that I extract form the stories of Aesop using fables in his own life; be your own advocate and use the fable form of short stories to advance your cause and save your hide, and, as is the very point of this whole book – to make a salient point and convey a lesson!

From Thomas Newbegging's translation:

"Even when a slave, readiness of resource was a characteristic of Æsop, and often stood him in good stead. His first master, Demarchus, one day brought home some choice figs, which he handed to his butler, telling him that he would partake of them after his bath. The butler had a friend paying him a visit, and by way of entertainment placed the figs before him, and both heartily partook of them. Fearing the displeasure of Demarchus, he resolved to charge Æsop with the theft. Having finished his ablutions, Demarchus ordered the fruit to be brought; but the butler had none to bring, and charged Æsop with having stolen and eaten them. The slave, being summoned, denied the charge. It was a serious matter for one in his position. To be guilty meant many stripes, if not death. He begged to have some warm water, and he would prove his innocence. The water being brought, he took a deep drink; then, putting his finger down his gullet, the water—the sole contents of his stomach—was belched. Demarchus now ordered the butler to do the same, with the result that he was proved to be both thief and liar and was punished accordingly.

Philosopher notwithstanding, Xanthus appears to have been often in hot water. On another occasion his wife left him, whether on account of her bad temper (as the report goes), or from his too frequent indulgence in liquor, matters little. He was anxious that she should return, but how to induce her was a difficulty hard to compass. Æsop, as usual, was equal to it. 'Leave it to me, master!' said he. Going to market, he gave orders to this dealer and that and the other, to send of their best to the residence of Xanthus, as, being about to take unto himself another wife, he intended to celebrate the happy occasion by a feast. The report spread like wildfire, and coming to the ears of his spouse, she quickly gathered up her belongings in the place where she had taken up her abode, and returned to the house of her lord and master. 'Take another wife, say you, Xanthus! Not whilst I am alive, my dear!' And so, the ruse was successful, for, as the story affirms, she settled down to her duties, and no further cause for separation occurred between them ever after."

I believe it's important, as a fabulist yourself, to develop an appreciation for the spontaneous storytelling skills of Aesop. You'll need not become Aesop, but Aesopian in your style. Aesop's master, Xandrus, was always in hot water with his wife, or he'd stumble into problems among his colleagues.

On another occasion his wife left him, whether on account of her bad temper (as the report goes), or from his too frequent indulgence in liquor (as is not unlikely), matters little. He was anxious that she should return, but how to induce her was a difficulty hard to compass. Æsop, as usual, was equal to it. 'Leave it to me, master!' said he. Going to market, he gave orders to this dealer and that and the other, to send of their best to the residence of anthus, as, being about to take unto himself another wife, he intended to celebrate the happy occasion by a feast. The report spread like wildfire, and coming to the ears of his spouse, she quickly gathered up her belongings in the place where she had taken up her abode, and returned to the house of her lord and master. 'Take another wife, say you, anthus! Not whilst I am alive, my dear!' And so, the ruse was successful, for, as the story affirms, she settled down to her duties, and no further cause for separation occurred between them ever after.

Early literature tells of a few erotic fables told by Aesop concerning Xandrus's wife seducing the witty man and making a bargain for ten rendezvous. His reward for his services, from the seductress, was to be a new shirt. After nine hookups, she reneged on the deal and Aesop protested a bit too loudly. Xandrus found them arguing and inquired. Aesop explained "your wife asked me to pluck ten apples from the orchard, promising me a shirt. After tossing a stone at the nine, she announced she was happy and did not need another." There are more. You see, his fables were not told for children.

Aesop, so the story goes, was mute until graced with the gift of speech after which time he spun fables to survive and to advance his standing. There are many resources about Aesop's life in ancient times, as author Laura Gibbs cites in *Aesop's Fables, A New Translation,* by Oxford World's Classics. To the extent we need to know from whence our good hero storyteller hales, Gibbs offers this, taken from an unattributed Greek novel, *The Life of Aesop,* written in the first century:

> "Aesop, our great benefactor, the storyteller, chanced to be a slave, and by birth he was a Phrygian from Phrygia. He was extremely ugly to look at, filthy with a big fat belly, and a big fat head, snub-nosed, misshapen, dark skinned, dwarfish, flatfooted, squint-eyed, and in short, a freak of nature." (Rather harsh I would say). Gibbs says he was mute and unable to speak…until the goddess Isis rewarded him with the gift of speech after the kindness he had shown.

Many Aesopian scholars dispute his ugliness. It is unimportant, so let's embrace that handsome guy, that loveable image cast in sculpture and on canvas. Embrace his inner beauty and his stories!

Robert Martel

Who Was This Legend Called Aesop?

From all accounts, he was a revered storyteller who lived 600 years before Christ, as you know by now. His fabulous fables did not make it to the printed page for an estimated 300 years after his death! This, as you might guess, left lots of time for his oral stories to be adjusted for the times, and he was credited with some fables which he did not invent. Nonetheless, regardless of the originator, we are blessed with hundreds of fables with lessons for our times. It is assumed today, and for as far back to the earlier days of Aesop's Fables having spread throughout the land, that people today are familiar with his magical stories. It is a pretty safe assumption, yet if you are a professional hypnotist using his fables in your transformational change work, then I suggest you ask, then explain, just to be safe. (I am always saddened to learn that many of my adult clients were never exposed to the works of Aesop nor did their parents read much to them as a child. I always encourage my clients to read Aesop's Fables and I usually gift them a copy of an illustrated version upon completion of our work together.)

Back in the day, you know, the early days of philosophy, education, written language, and the search for meaning, 'one was supposed to be kept up on their Aesop' and familiar with the morals of the stories.

Heradotus, the Greek historian, attested around 500 BCE that Aesop was already widespread in classical Greece. Although this was prior to any written form of his fables, Aristophanes, the Greek comedic playwright, made the basic assumption that everyone in earshot of his plays was at least familiar if not well versed in the legend, Aesop. To be Aesopian in your philosophical discussions was almost required in Greek society at that time.

In fact, in his 414 BCE play *The Birds,* Aristophanes mentions Aesop on two occasions, referencing two separate fables. Aesop says that the crested lark was the first bird to be created, even before Gaia, the Earth. As a result, when the lark's father became sick and died, there was no earth to bury him in. On the fifth day that his body had been lying there, the frustrated lark, not knowing what else to do, buried her father in her own head.

In each scene mentioning Aesop, Pithetaerus says to Euelepides, the two main characters:

PITHETAERUS (referencing the Lark and her Crest)

"That's because you are ignorant and heedless, and have never read your Aesop. He is the one who tells us that the lark was born before all other creatures, indeed before the Earth; his father died of sickness, but the Earth did not exist then; he remained unburied for five days, when the bird in its dilemma decided, for want of a better place, to entomb its father in its own head."

And later in the play:

PITHETAERUS (referencing The Fox and the Eagle)

Remember Aesop's fables. It is told there that the fox fared very badly, because he had made an alliance with the eagle.

If you enjoy good writing, I encourage you to read Aristophanes' play. *The Birds* won critical acclaim in its day as a perfectly told fantasy remarkably notable for its mimicry of birds and the songs performed by the chorus. Go find it at classics.mit.edu or your favorite ancient literary source. (It's a story that follows Pithetaerus, a middle-aged Athenian who persuades the world's birds to create a new city in the sky (thereby gaining control over all communications between men and gods), and is himself eventually miraculously transformed into a bird-like god figure, and replaces Zeus as the pre-eminent power in the cosmos.)

Getting to the background of this mystery and possibly mythical author, Aesop, credited with penning so many fabulous stories, I offer this synopsis taken from the public domain version of the book *The Talking Beasts,* at Gutenburg.org:

> *How shall I bring to your mind the time and distance that separate us from the Age of Fable? Think of what seemed to you the longest week of your life. Think of fifty-two of these in a year; then think of two thousand five hundred years and try to realize that Aesop—sometimes called the Eighth Wise Man—lived twenty-five centuries ago and made these wonderful tales that delight us to-day.*

> *Shakespeare is even yet something of a mystery, although he was born in our own era, less than five hundred years ago; but men are still trying to discover any new facts of his life that might better explain his genius. A greater mystery is grand old Homer, who has puzzled the world for centuries. Scholars are not certain whether the "Iliad" or "Odyssey" are the work of one or more than one mind. Who can say? for the thrilling tales were told—probably after the fashion of all the minstrels of his day—more than eight hundred years before Christ.*

> *On the background of that dim distant long ago, perhaps two hundred years later than Homer, looms the magnificent figure of another mysterious being—Aesop the Greek slave.*

> *Wherever and whenever he lived, and whether, in fact, he ever lived at all, he seems very real to us, even though more*

than two thousand years have passed. Among all the stories that scholars and historians have told of him—sifting through the centuries the true from the false—we get a vivid picture of the man. He was born in Greece, probably in Phrygia, about 620 years before Christ. He had more than one master and it was the last, Iadmon, who gave him his liberty because of his talents and his wisdom. The historian Plutarch recounts his presence at the court of Croesus, King of Lydia, and his meeting Thales and Solon there, telling us also that he reproved the wise Solon for discourtesy toward the king. Aesop visited Athens and composed the famous fable of Jupiter and the Frogs for the instruction of the citizens. Whether he left any written fables is very uncertain, but those known by his name were popular in Athens when that city was celebrated throughout the world for its wit and its learning. Both Socrates and Plato delighted in them; Socrates, we read, having amused himself during the last days of his life with turning into verse some of Aesop's "myths" as he called them. Think of Socrates conning these fables in prison four hundred years before Christ, and then think of a more familiar picture in our own day—a gaunt, dark-faced, black-haired boy poring over a book as he lay by the fireside in a little Western farmhouse; for you remember that Abraham Lincoln's literary models were "Aesop's Fables," "The Pilgrim's Progress" and the Bible. Perhaps he read the fable of the Fig Tree, Olive, Vine, and Bramble from the ninth chapter of Judges, or that of the Thistle and Cedar from the fourteenth chapter of II Kings and noted that teaching by story-telling was still well in vogue six hundred years after Aesop.

I share the above, from The Talking Beasts, which was published in 1922 and available at the Gutenberg Project. It is a great compendium of fables from Aesop and other greats. While this book is all things Aesop, if you exhaust yourself in applying his fables or if you seek morals from other cultures you will not be disappointed by consulting this resource.

Now Let's Meet Two Great Men Who Never Met Each Other

Once upon a time there were two great minds that influenced the people of their time and beyond.

One lived 600 years before Christ, the other lived in the 20th century. Both very witty with a humor that presents a lesson and both exceptional masters of the story as a therapeutic tool. Two people with the same fundamental approach to influence, the indirect suggestion or moral found within a short metaphorical story, often in the form of a fable. Each a pioneer. Both offering powerful insights to better our lives by influencing the subconscious mind through hypnotic storytelling.

Aesop meet Erickson

Milton Hyland Erickson was a pioneer in the field of hypnotherapy, well known for his creativity, his superb use of language, and his ability to meet the patient (client) where they were in life and use that as the leverage point for change. He worked extemporaneously with what was presented. Aesop was a pioneer in telling stories with metaphors, using the animal world to convey a moral; a lesson for life in which the attentive reader would glean its value and take from it the meaning it would apply. Aesop, too, was quick-witted in using on-the-spot, instant fables to get a point across or influence those around him.

Erickson defined hypnosis as "the evocation and utilization of unconscious learnings." Based on his writings, he believed that we were in closest harmony with our own inner knowledge and wisdom, and in the best possible rapport when client and hypnotist were in a 'shared trance' state. Essentially, I take this as a subconscious-to-subconscious communication experience and is the epitome of the hypnotist being 'with the client' and participating in the change work undertaken.

Milton H. Erickson was the master metaphorical storyteller, and remains so, to the point that his methods should be studied and practiced by all professionals in the business of change work. Erickson loved using metaphors and stories. They are a great way to deepen the hypnotic state. Aesop's Fables and the fables you will introduce in a clinical setting will certainly indicate that you are indeed becoming a proficient Ericksonian Aesopian practitioner.

But, since this book is not a book about Ericksonian hypnosis, per se, I refer you to author Richard Nongard's excellent, easy to comprehend book on the subject, *Speak Ericksonian*. He takes the mystery out of trying to understand Erickson. Start there, with his book, where he will lead you to additional respected resources if you seek to master the Ericksonian style of hypnosis work. This book is, however, about learning to speak Aesopian with an Ericksonian approach to clinical application of a good story. Erickson would encourage you today to be more Aesopian in your work, as you discover how to move towards more effective storytelling methods, as you grow in your journey as a professional hypnotist and a teacher.

So, let's get on with it!

Are you starting to channel Aesop yet? He was, of course, one of the world's most famous and celebrated storytellers, perhaps both in his time, and up until this very moment. Blend Aesop and Erickson and you will consistently be the sought-after professional! I wonder, if you are curious as well, whether he even realized the impact would have on the world, his stories passed down through the ages.

The Influence of Aesop

To begin to appreciate the power of fables, as the story goes, Demades, a famous Greek orator, was once addressing an assembly at Athens on a subject of great importance, and in vain tried to fix the attention of his hearers. They laughed among themselves, watched the sports of the children, and in twenty other ways showed their want of interest in the subject of the discourse.

Demades, after a short pause, spoke as follows:

> "Ceres one day journeyed in company with a Swallow and an Eel." At this there was marked attention and every ear strained now to catch the words of the orator. "The party came to a river," continued he; "the Eel swam across, and the Swallow flew over." He then resumed the subject of his harangue.
>
> A great cry, however, arose from the people, "And Ceres? and Ceres?" cried they. "What did Ceres do?"
>
> "Why, the goddess was, as she is now," replied he, "mightily offended that people should have their ears open to any sort of foolery and shut to words of truth and wisdom."

As such, the power of a story with a lesson-for-life message was powerfully demonstrated. Such are the skills of a good storyteller. Good hypnotic storytelling comes from the story itself and your natural voice that passionately delivers a memorable lesson.

The Art of Hypnotic Storytelling

While this subject is a book in and of itself, I touch upon it briefly here to help you appreciate the fable from the listener or reader's standpoint. Simply connect with that magical ability of yours to persuade and influence, as you do with the power of your hypnotic suggestions in client sessions. Channel that inner storyteller! (That is what that this book is really about!)

The task of your client is finding the meaning, assigning, and connecting to the deeper message of the fable. Of course, you know that establishing rapport is the first step. I am referring to a deepening of the effective rapport you already establish with your clients in your clinical practice; building deep trust and confidence as you work *with* them to make strides and realize goals or resolve issues. Just as they need to trust the process of clinical hypnosis work with you, they need to also trust your words and guidance. So, find the common ground by sharing how you have used the lessons of Aesop's Fables in your own life, or how you've helped others, even if you have to make it a tall tale! I would add that timing is important in introducing a fable into the clinical process – but do it! It's magical. Be prepared for the naysayer who dismisses Aesop's Fables. More on that later. Be committed to helping them hear the voice of Aesop and using your own magical words to involve them in the process!

In preparing listeners to hear your fable story, rapport-building is essential, as are solid communication skills. Look for the signs that deep rapport is present. Here are 7 quick tips for rapport-building as it relates to storytelling, as shared by James Hazlerig, Master Storyteller and Hypnotist, who so graciously wrote the foreword to this book.

A Storyteller's Seven Tips for Rapport-Building

1. Introduce your story by relating it to something in the conversation leading up to it, or to something that you know about your audience/client.
2. Visualize your story as you tell it. Describe what you 'see' with your mind's eye.
3. Engage your body in the telling. Don't be afraid to assign locations to characters or objects by 'looking' at them.
4. Make eye-contact about 50 to 75% of the time.
5. Engage your voice in the telling. You don't have to do dramatically different voices for each character—though you can, especially with children—but you can vary your pitch, tone, and speed for dramatic effect.
6. Engage your facial expressions in the telling. Allow your face to momentarily convey the emotions of characters or the observer as you tell your story.
7. Be subtle. Use all of these tools gently and sparingly, 'turning up the volume' on your performance only as quickly as your audience comes along. You will know the audience is engaged by their reactions; many will become 'spellbound': glazed eyes, slow breath, stillness. Others will react physically to events in the story, perhaps recoiling at unpleasant parts or leaning into the magic.

Find James Hazlerig on the web at

www.hypnoticstorytellingcourse.com.

Applying Hypnotic Language Patterns in the Fables

Like you, Aesop was a master influencer and persuader.

While words certainly matter as you study the language of Aesop's fables, you might notice that you are becoming more hypnotic in your everyday language. You will also start seeing new potential fables, and you will probably start spinning micro-fables straight from the language patterns and words your client offers while in session with you. It is about telling the story effectively, not about perfection as ancient fabulists may suggest. Choosing the right words is important, however, in presenting the notion of being Aesopian in the quest for client progress.

Pro Tip: Nothing sells like believing in what you are saying to others, actually picturing the very success they seek, focused as they are, in the zone, subconsciously with them in the moment as you are in hypnosis together, at least if you are doing it well! So, as you examine and construct hypnotic language patterns, it is your *belief and passion* that will shine through as you speak Aesopian with your clients. Much as the fable lowers resistance to the moral of the story, your professional enthusiasm for the use of fables will lower their resistance to using such stories for their subconscious mind to absorb.

He probably did not realize, maybe he did after all, but perhaps Aesop was wiser than we even realize, and he was a master hypnotist to be sure. His witty fables made him a freedman and thus opened up new opportunities as he entertained Xandrus' friends. His fables also freed him from prison. Unfortunately, his last attempts at fables, as the story goes, failed to prevent the incensed Delphinians from tossing him into the sea. But his final fables did work in that they conveyed a lesson for the citizens of Delphi, as they felt extreme guilt for killing an honorable man and it led to the demise of Delphi itself. Have you drawn the parallel? Just as Aesop told fables throughout his life, ultimately for his freedom, your clients will enjoy freedom from what ails them as their subconscious mind

Once someone is open to hearing a good story the rest is easy. Sometimes a client may resist the very idea that a children's story could help them. I once had a client say, "If all I needed was a copy of Aesop's Fables, then why did you not say so at the onset?" Of course, she was amazingly surprised at just how easy it was to remove herself from the issue she wanted to address and observe unattached. There is something powerful about the advice served up by an animal character in a story, or a talking tree. (That concept is proven every day in the hypnotic marketing stories we are told by animals and fictitious characters!)

The great news about using fables is you can incorporate them with your current clinical approach, whether it be direct hypnosis and neuro-linguistic programming (NLP), or a more indirect style. You can compound suggestions, subtly or overtly, to spark change and open their mind to the receptive process of hearing new ideas. Hypnotic language patterns may become important in helping to convince or persuade the client to 'play along' with your Aesopian hypnosis!

I have created a couple of examples to share, about other clients who may have resisted a fable as a tool for their mind to embrace. You can do the same! Apply selected hypnotic language patterns in a story or to convince someone of the value in making time to read Aesop's Fables. Consider this hypnotic language pattern as shared by author and hypnotist Karen Hand, in her newsletter:

> *"That word "YOU" is like music to your ears, is it not? "YOU" is the second most attention-getting word in our language. The first is your name. Persuasion is about using words/phrases strategically to focus awareness and calibrate success ... In Hypnosis patter, you are probably already aware of the effectiveness of the phrase, "YOU can do it, can YOU not?" ... The listener/client clearly understands the message is meant for them. "YOU can relax your eyelids so much they just stay closed ... only YOU can*

do it! No one can do it for YOU ... and when YOU are convinced YOU have relaxed the eyelids so much; they just stay closed ... check them."

This is a permissive direct suggestion. I wonder how you could use the above language pattern to suggest that your client actually open their mind ... and actually listen or read some fables. I've used this phrase with great success: *"I wonder whether you will be the type of person, like so many others I've worked with, to embrace the very idea of a fable as a tool in your process of making progress. Because it is so important, simply tell your subconscious mind 'stand by to cooperate' and then you can step aside and let your childlike mind hear what you ultimately want it to hear. You can do that, right?"*

Karen is masterful. "What happens when YOU can change just one word in your self-talk and restore your personal power for success? Read the next paragraph aloud and with passion:

"I know the truth. Only I can do it. I can celebrate my progress by claiming ownership of my behaviors ... (the good, the bad and the ugly) and I can confidently say, "I've got this! I can do anything I put my mind to doing!"

That is empowering, as she states in her newsletter. Apply appropriate specifics as necessary, to modify her language pattern for your client. Help them empower themselves with better self-talk. Help them reframe their situation and build self-confidence as you help them channel Aesop in the process.

In discussing this book with Karen, she offered these insights:

You probably already know that suggestions, hypnotic or not, are just as easily taken as ignored. And the client/listener makes the decision about what gets through to jive with a current belief or to become a new belief. Only the

65

listener/reader/client can do it. You cannot do it for them. But you can choose a variety of suggestions for encouragement. Notice the example suggestions can be used alone or as a 'script' for this goal.

Research shows that we retain information easily when we learn it in story form or metaphor.

I wonder if you have discovered yourself yet in Aesop's Fables.

You can easily remember those 'mommyisms' about 'crying wolf' or 'what the early bird gets', can you not?

A client once told me they got a pocket-sized edition of some great fables from Aesop, and they would read them periodically during the day to relax. And he winked when he remembered how much the stories apply to his own daily struggles and successes.

I don't know if you choose to read Aesop's Fables all the way through ... or if you choose to read the stories occasionally for a break ...or if you have your own plan for using the wisdom of Aesop ... but you can plan your own successful journey into the storybook of life, now.

In other words, when you know the goal/outcome it is a simple plug and play into hypnotic patter. In this example, I used some easy language patterns found in my book and plugged in Bob's goal of encouraging his clients to read the fables for their own good.

You can easily do the very same thing. And the more you practice putting the stated outcome into the patterns, the more you will feel comfortable in making any suggestions.

Words matter. They are the lifeblood of our profession! If you want to develop your influence and persuasion skills further, you could become an NLP master practitioner, but I want to give you the secret to fast-tracking your skills development. I recommend that you grab Karen's book *Magic Words and Language Patterns: The Hypnotist's Essential Guide to Crafting Irresistible Suggestions*. She can be reached at www.karenhand.com or find the book on-line..

I wonder which fables will resonate with your clients, and I wonder which ones are your favorites. Most importantly, however, I wonder how you will inspire your client to open their mind to the fable as a hypnotic tool to help them access their inner resources states of wisdom.

Here are several hypnotic language patterns that you might include in your repertoire. Notice how I have combined (for compounding effect) a couple of proven language patterns. Here are three that I use to suggest the value of a good story (aside from the stories I tell in a pre-talk with the client):

- *I wonder if it is time for you to tell your subconscious mind to <u>stand by to cooperate</u> ... for your highest and best .... as you allow your subconscious mind to step forward to hear what it needs to hear from you – your conscious intention ... opening your mind to new ideas ... as you already believe in the ability to do that inner change work ... and sometimes ... we just need to mindfully acknowledge the stories we tell ourselves ... and stories we may have forgotten ... or never enjoyed hearing ... <u>because</u> sometimes it is in a good story we find the meaning we need for our own purposes in any given moment .... and so far ... in what I've heard from you ... I may suggest a story or two for you to consider reading*

... or I may share here in a future session ... would that be ok? (Voila, you gain permission to suggest Aesop!)

- *I find ... in using hypnosis to help my clients find that spark and the courage to change, that <u>a person is able to</u> discover and apply meaningful changes if she wants them and make them permanent ... for all of the right reasons within ... <u>especially because you simply</u> want to do it for <u>yourself</u> ... and sometimes ... through a good hypnotic story ... such as Aesop's fables ... as one example ... I find that a person is <u>able</u> ... to understand that sooner or later ... as time passes and your mind absorbs new perspectives ... some lessons and morals we heard long ago ... or even newly discovered ... just make so much sense! <u>I wonder</u> .... <u>If you can imagine</u> ... if you'll give yourself permission to imagine just what Aesop has to say about you ... who knew that a guy who lived almost 3,000 years ago could help you find the magic key?*

- *As Henry Ford once said ... if you believe that you can or if you believe you cannot, you are right .... <u>A person ... any person</u> deserves to give themselves an opportunity to pause and see the world of possibilities around them ... possibilities that deserve new thinking ... because, as Einstein once said problems cannot be solved using the same mindset that created them ... and so, <u>if you want to</u> enjoy the benefits of the change you seek ... <u>then realize</u> you can enjoy them rather quickly. It may amaze you what a rapid shift in mindset can do for you ... when you allow the shift to happen and just let that new you emerge. I cannot do it for you ... so long as you want it ... you may allow the Magic of Aesop to help you make true progress. What happens for you when you first <u>imagine</u> the feeling of feeling that the shift is* *already happening ... and that the decisions and actions you want to take ... start happening?*

Practice using these language patterns and decide to become a student of hypnotic language patterns. Heck! Use them to be a better communicator, a better parent, a more effective leader. As Karen says in her book, learning to use your voice tone and inflection are the hidden secret to maximizing your effectiveness. You do not need to be a voice-over artist or master storyteller ... just speak naturally with the right pace, volume, annunciation, and pronunciation as you would like to enjoy, too.

Let's Apply the Milton Model: Powerful Language Patterns

In studying Milton H. Erickson, Bandler and Grinder gave birth to the Milton Model which, as Richard Nongard says in his book, *Speak Ericksonian,* consist of certain "language patterns that are intended to focus a person's attention to create an internal experience" designed to help them realize they have the inner power to tap into that vast resource we call the subconscious mind. Kevin Hogan, the master of Covert Hypnosis teaches such subtleties, as I am sure Erickson would be proud, that the language patterns would hardly be detectible in a hypnotic conversation. It is about eliciting a response from the client, compliance that their subconscious mind somehow cannot resist *considering*. It is not about manipulation. Hypnotic language patterns when used ethically, for a noble purpose, are simply a tool to help the client do the inner change work. It is always about their change and what they want for themselves. This is what makes the introduction of Aesop's Fables so right for the client. With your expert assistance, you are enabling the client to subconsciously connect with Aesop's words.

Pro Tip: Compound your success and that of the client as you apply hypnotic language patterns as needed, along with your use of

Aesop's Fables in a clinical setting. Separately, they both achieve a lowering of resistance to suggestions. Together, the storytelling and the language patterns combine to increase the likelihood that a behavioral or experiential response will occur, or an internal realization will take place.

It is not the goal of this book to teach the Milton Method. I simply wanted to shine a light on the subject and call attention to his work. The process of Ericksonian hypnosis is intentionally vague, allowing the mind to adapt and adopt suggestions on their terms in a way that makes sense to them. It is not about commanding the client to do as told! In this vagueness, it is not always so easy to see where an Ericksonian hypnosis session starts or ends!

Here are three additional compounded suggestions I use, from the Milton Model, to guide the client along to either opening their mind to the Aesopian hypnosis process or to simply hear an Aesopian moral that you interject in hypnotic conversation.

- *I wonder ... <u>can you really enjoy</u> the feeling now of taking a nice breath ... the best deep breath you can take ... and simply relaxing deeper ... and as you do so ... ask yourself <u>what happens when you</u> ... begin to visualize and connect with the feeling of progress you seek .... Sometime ...when it is the right time ... you'll feel the alignment of your whole mind ... and suddenly the solution starts to seem so clear. Sometimes a good old Aesop's fable can accelerate that realization ...*

- *Now <u>I want you to</u> consider this ... as your mind becomes more receptive as you relax more ... now <u>you don't have to understand</u> how a good story does its magic ... in order to use it in any way that seems right ... <u>because</u> sometimes a good story is just plain enjoyable ... you don't have to try* *whatsoever... and you even do not have to do it at all if you don't want to! Let the child within you see if an Aesop's fable might just be right for you right now ... <u>many a person has shifted </u>and transformed their behavior because a simple story changed their view.*

- *Think about this ...<u> you might want</u> to take a small step forward .... <u>now</u>. <u>I'm curious</u> as I suppose you are as well ... about whether you decide right now ... or perhaps maybe you'll <u>eventually</u> realize you are able to take back control and use self-hypnosis to connect with a fable or two. There is a part of you that is already noticing the shift that you are allowing yourself to enjoy.*

You will find your own language that propels your client to a state of acceptance to your process. Fables are such an easy sell but when someone resists you might have to pull out all the stops. As we close this chapter, know that you are building the skills for becoming a great Aesopian hypnotist. I wonder just how amazed you will be when you start to see how easy your job becomes as you listen with a tuned ear for using fables in your work. No, they are not always required but they sure do help you make that subconscious mind connection.

I know you are anxious to jump into the fables. Trust my process. We will get you there. Keep in mind, too, I have written this book as a reference. We are building the foundation so you can magically, effortlessly and quite automatically be that fabulous hypnotic fabulist.

Chapter Three:
Walking A Welcoming Path Forward

"The mind, once stretched by a new idea, never returns to its original dimensions."

Ralph Waldo Emerson

Let us take a short break from Aesop and focus on your client. In the next chapter we will swing around again and focus on the fable and how hypnotic stories will help achieve magical results.

I am calling this my 'departure chapter' as it may seem apart from the promise of the book. Trust the process, as we tell our clients! It is intended to help with your framework for being an effective Aesopian hypnotist. This chapter may seem a bit tangential, I will admit, but the objective is to share some concepts I use in the office to help clients. Remember, the best professional hypnotist is with the client, subconscious minds working together. So, this chapter is offered to help you be most effective as a hypnotic storytelling practitioner, deepening rapport and connecting with the client as you introduce Aesop's Fables as a clinical tool. The idea here is that you will take away at least one tool to add to your repertoire. I hope you find it helpful.

I am sure by now that you realize that fables, indeed, play a role in the emotional healing that enables a person to live a happier and more fulfilling life. The lessons from Aesop's fables, and so many of the stories passed down through generations, help people find more positive ways of dealing with their feelings. As you read more, let me stretch your imagination to ask you this: *I wonder if you could examine the fables on a whole new level as you strive to work with your clients ... and imagine for a moment ... what if the animals in Aesop's fables had feelings, too, and needed to make an appointment to see you for hypnotic change work? Just wondering what that might look like for you? Imagine a fox, eagle, crow, lion, donkey, ant, frog, grasshopper or even Aesop himself sitting in your office. Wouldn't that be cool?*

Onward!

In my practice, I always use the metaphor of the welcoming path, something I have developed along the way as a metaphor for the journey of life. I will talk about the choice they have of walking it backwards, always living and looking back down the timeline of their past, or they can pivot and face their present reality and also choose to live hypnotically. The path, as I explain and suggest in hypnosis, connotes a certain sense of calmness and relief, I suppose. Clients connect with the metaphor and find a sense of peace within as they choose the right path for themselves, moving forward. For me, it first came to mind in reading *The Miracle of Mindfulness* by Thich Nat Hahn, Buddhist Monk, as he wrote from exile in Paris to his brother in Vietnam. Mindfully walking a meditative path, whether in actuality, or in the magical mind using mental rehearsal and visualization is a healing experience that gives comfort and hope. I hope you will embrace it, both for your clients and for yourself!

A brief definition is perhaps appropriate here. Quite simply, as defined by Jon Kabat-Zinn, mindfulness is essentially paying attention on purpose with greater awareness and without judgement. Further, as Greater Good says at their Berkely.edu program:

> " *Mindfulness means maintaining a moment-by-moment awareness of our thoughts, feelings, bodily sensations, and surrounding environment, through a gentle, nurturing lens.*
>
> *Mindfulness also involves acceptance, meaning that we pay attention to our thoughts and feelings without judging them—without believing, for instance, that there is a "right" or "wrong" way to think or feel in a given moment. When we practice mindfulness, our thoughts tune into what we are sensing in the present moment rather than rehashing the past or imagining the future.*
>
> *Though it has its roots in Buddhist meditation, a secular practice of mindfulness has entered the American mainstream in recent years, in part through the work of Jon Kabat-Zinn and his Mindfulness-Based Stress Reduction (MBSR) program, which he launched at the University of Massachusetts Medical School in 1979. Since that time, thousands of studies have documented the physical and mental health benefits of mindfulness in general and MBSR in particular, inspiring countless programs to adapt the MBSR model for schools, prisons, hospitals, veterans centers, and beyond.*"

My own two cents on mindfulness?

Mindfulness is not a new concept. Long before the mindfulness movement of the 1980s, and the explosion of mindfulness gurus on the Internet today, mindfulness was being cultivated by the great philosophers of past centuries. Epictetus, Seneca, and Markus Aurelius have much to say on the subject as they were teaching a way of living our daily lives. And others preceded them! Decide to be a mindful Aesopian (and Ericksonian) hypnotist. Walk your own mindfulness path. Look into the books by Yapko, Kabat-Zinn, and even Victor Frankl's book: *Man's Search for Meaning*, which is essentially a meditation on what the gruesome experience of Auschwitz taught him about the primary purpose of life: the quest for meaning. For Frankl, meaning came from three possible sources: purposeful work, love, and courage in the face of difficulty. What say you?

Ah, back to the Welcoming Path!

In the office I will ask my client to envision a path, something they can see themselves walking on, enjoying a walking meditation in the right direction, whatever that means to them in the moment. The obstacles and opportunities along the way will present a chance for their growth mindset to develop as they, with an open mind, are able to see self-learnings along the way. I will often say:

> *"Isn't it nice to know, finally, you are taking even the smallest of steps along this right path at this moment in your life? I can only imagine that your journey has taken you on other paths ... and aren't we all on a journey back, anyway? A journey from the time of our birth, back to our creator ... the human life so fragile ... and dependent on the loving care of others until and sometimes far after we reach adulthood ... and yet that child within us is always alive yet somehow dormant at times, for whatever reason ... as you walk this path, imagine you are carrying a rucksack full of stones ...*

*and as you relax with every healing breath ... you reach in
and toss aside one stone ... feeling what it feels like to walk
a little lighter ... more erect ... feeling in more control and
feeling more peace within you with each stone you cast aside
... let those stones be your letting go of whatever is holding
you back ...*

I offer those words as a nice preamble as it sets the stage for introducing a variety of things along the welcoming path as they take bold courageous, deliberate steps forward, just like the tortoise! Modify and enjoy as you wish. I will add metaphors and similes based on what the client has expressed, and suggest other 'signposts' along the way, all to help with the journey. I also will say, *"hey, you are doing great! You got this! You must feel awesome with what you are accomplishing!"* Then I let them own those new feelings. Remember, only they can walk the path. You cannot do it for them. It is all about the choices they make for themselves. I always give clients the book, *As A Man Thinketh*, a classic from the early twentieth century. It teaches that our present moment life is, for the most part, a product of the choices we have made along the way.

Full disclosure, the welcoming path hit me square between the eyes when my good friend and colleague, and one of my hypnosis instructors, Patricia MacIsaac of Southshore Hypnosis in Hingham, MA, took me through a very impactful hypnotic journey whereby, in a spiritual dowsing session, Jesus appeared in a garden, knelt and handed me a rose and reaffirmed that He wanted me doing this work for Him. I have held that experience since and it fuels my passion for this wonderful profession. Reminds me of the Gospel song, The Garden. Cue Elvis.

Planning Your Fabulous Fable Telling

Ask yourself, as you learn the details of the client's case, how will you help them apply the lessons of Aesop's Fables to their life and toward making progress as they walk that welcoming path? It comes with experience as your confidence grows as a storyteller.

You've probably gathered from reading fables, that the characters in a fable become allies and resources along the welcoming path, creating a safety net of sorts. The welcoming path itself becomes a resource! I anchor their feelings and connect to being on that path, bringing them back to the feeling of being in more control of their emotions, thoughts and actions. With each step forward along the path, a sensation of greater self-confidence arrives, reaffirming the decision to choose a new direction. The path provides a connection, as a labyrinth does, allowing the client to explore and experience what they need in order to get what they need. And, as the last words my mother shared with me before passing *"Bobby, it's okay to fall down, so long as you remember to fall forward. That way, you are always making progress."* There's a fable to be told here somewhere. Maybe she got it from her Irish mother who got it from her Irish mother who was told by a leprechaun or gypsy princess ... or maybe it's something she got from the hypnotist who helped her stop smoking decades earlier. Perhaps she got it from one of Aesop's fables!

Connecting with the Executive Director Within

Imagine now, how you can add fable characters to your client's walk along the welcoming path, or how you can help them access their own resources to read and find fables that resonate. Imagine adding fable characters along the path for the client to consult. I wonder what the fox would tell your client who is struggling with an emotional issue. Would he offer advice for getting unstuck and reference a fable? You get the idea. The client will assign the value!

In the end, perhaps the single most important point of this book is that your work as a fabulist and Aesopian hypnotist is to help the client increase the awareness of the stories they are living now and how to 'tell a better story' to themselves as they become more mindful of the power of a story – positive and negative – and how their new choices and decision opportunities will (or will not) open new doors. New beliefs lead to new feelings and new directions, allowing them to unlock a better future and chart their destiny. Read this paragraph a couple of more times before proceeding. It's central to the thesis of this book and is the context for adding fables to your practice work and for accelerated client progress.

Here's an example of what I mean, something I use (after induction and deepener):

"As you continue to walk this path ... in your mind right now and in reality, I suppose ... and what is reality anyway ... A perception at the moment. Well ... as you breath and relax more ... know that reality shifts as our mind suspends disbelief and allows new ideas to be considered .... And ... each day ... you are ... feeling more confident in your own abilities and connected to that authentic you that resides deep in your mind ... more fully aware that every day and in every way you are better and better ... better at relaxing ... and about your new abilities to stay calm, relaxed and in control ... as others experience, you, too may realize an epiphany ... or not ... but you do bring the morals of Aesop's Fables ... as they pertain ... and as they give support and courage ... that you can do anything you put your mind to ... and so ... image you ... taking a rest along the past ... a reflective and rejuvenating rest ... maybe you see a comforting place to sit for a moment ... a rock ... a tree stump ... or whatever you imagine as restful in this moment ... maybe a place to

pause and breathe a few relaxing breaths and get that relaxation response going ... and I wonder if, like others have reported ... you can connect with your favorite animal character from your favorite Aesop's Fable? .... perhaps the sly fox, the brave lion, the observant mouse, the crow, eagle or any of the others that may pop into your mind ... and as you connect with those issues you are mulling over ... the things perhaps that are holding you back ... I wonder if your mind starts to offer up solutions ... perhaps morals from fables ... Or suggestions your subconscious mind knows are right for you but you've held off any action ... and you know ... that action ... is the key. Maybe you simply need to open your mind and heart and let the fable characters you meet along the way ... guide you to the right fables for you ... in this moment and the weeks ahead."

I created the above script shortly after opening my practice in 2009 to help a client end her sugar addiction. Without her even revealing the reasons she was letting the bad habit rule her life, I simply suggested she read a few of Aesop's fables to find the suggestions she needed. Bingo! She stopped consuming a 12-pack of Coca cola each day. When her mind was ready it assigned value to the story.

You see, I use Aesop's Fables as one component in the clinical hypnosis work. I will also add signposts for them to note along the way according to the feelings needing attention, while in hypnosis in the chair, sometimes in the style of the old, witty and sequential Burma Shave highway advertising. (Look it up!)

I may include such things as:

- You see a series of three road signs up ahead ... the first one reads, *"Every day and in every way, better and better at ...."* (self-talk, relaxing with anchors I've learnt to use, at letting go of the past and forgiving what needs forgiving) or... As you bring to mind a time you felt great about a really

important accomplishment ... a goal ... a project ... a
decision ... Now, I wonder ... if you can see ahead a
billboard on the side of the path ... and it reads ... <name>
you can do anything you put your mind to doing ... and for
all of the right reasons ... that sign becomes a part of your
fabric ... pause and reread it ... and think about your journey
... and how you want to feel leaving my office today ... and
knowing exactly your next step." You get the idea.

- Up ahead, *"you notice a person walking, apparently feeling
very happy-go-lucky and confident. It's you ... in the future
... and as you walk toward that new you ... I wonder if you
can begin to feel the way he/she feels having changed,
shifted ... and can you bring those feelings into you now ...
and act as if the future is already here ... and a new you is,
indeed, emerging."*

- I will often include: *"I wonder if you notice the sign pointing
to the labyrinth along the path you are walking? You may
know that a labyrinth is an excellent way to pause and enjoy
a healing, often spiritual journey within ... releasing what
needs to be released ... in the center, receiving what you
need to receive ... and existing ... reconnecting with self and
with your Creator, and the world itself ... you can decide if
exploring the labyrinth is right for you ... walk it when you
have time ..."*

- And finally, *for our purpose of example I often add:*
*"listening to the sounds of nature as you walk ... mindful of
things you may or may not be noticing in life around you as
well ... aware of the flowers, the birds singing to you ... you
hear a babbling brook and as you investigate it ... you find
a place to sit and enjoy the sounds of water flowing and
cascading over the rocks ... as you begin to connect with the*

peace and tranquility of this scene you also connect with your own authenticity ... a place where you can see, hear, touch, smell and experience in a multi-sensory way ... all that you need in order to achieve peace of mind with a better sense of progress ... create an anchor with me now ... so you can go to this place anytime you'd like...''

Your Client Owns the Progress, You Own the Process!

So, let me ask you. Who is in charge of making the change the client seeks, while on whatever journey they imagine? You're the expert. But the change work is theirs. You're providing the inspiration and motivation. They are providing the perspiration and decision-making.

Well, the client may try to assign that responsibility to the hypnotist, maybe expecting, initially, a wave of a magic wand to make troubles disappear. Wouldn't that be grand! Well, our job, as teacher, consultant and hypnotist, is to work with the client to help them find the right answer, the right motivation to change; to connect their intention, ultimately, with the right action that brings progress and results. At least, that is how I look at this honorable role as a professional hypnotist. And, if you are not a professional hypnotist, I have great news. This all still applies, for there is a part of you that plays the same role either internally for your own change work, or for gently helping others.

Every client (and every hypnotist, too) needs to face reality and channel their own inner resources, and that is, as I once learned from my 16-year-old son, 27 years ago, something I try to instill in each client as appropriate. Fables take the effort out of that requisite step.

"Dad, you have to be your own drill sergeant," my son shared with me at 16 years of age. "The world does not give a damn about you.

Life goes on," he said, "despite what is going on in your life. It is your life. Live it." Now, I did serve in the Navy for eight years, but he did not get such sage advice from me. It came from his Krav Maga instructors, I believe.

Ultimately, it comes down to self-accountability, and deciding if you are willing to do what you need to do in order to make progress on the presenting issue, or not. There is no 'try', only 'do' or 'do not'.

If you agree that the client walks in with the solution, and the 'script' for the change work is revealed by the client in the initial sessions (in most cases), then you might agree that the 'executive director' resides in the client's subconscious and is also influenced by the conscious intention of the individual. My point is that, even if the client has no clue why they are experiencing disempowering feelings, or even expressing what they are feeling, we can help them connect to that internal director and help them begin to see themselves taking back more control over their life. Seeing them accept this notion of self-accountability.

Imagine good old Aesop walking his own welcoming, mindful path, enjoying his walk toward freedom, spinning new life lessons as he walks!

Sometimes it's time to 'wash the dishes' or 'chop wood and carry water' as Thich Nat Hahn says in his book, *The Miracle of Mindfulness;* each a common metaphor meaning when it's time to do the work, then do the work and do the work well, with focus, attention and purpose.

Sometimes we must help even the best intended client to actually focus better. I'll often use the metaphor of a labyrinth to explain, as above, the phases of the hypnotic work while we are together and beyond. It helps. They need to release, receive, and reconnect with the world just as a labyrinth experience would demand, for the truly motivated person.

While living in the present moment of reality, accepting what is rather than what was or what could be, fable telling allows your client to safely travel back in time with you to 'hear what Aesop said' without necessarily having to face their own past (at this moment). Visualizing success, the very idea of picturing the goal achieved or life with the problem resolved and connecting to those feelings is the precursor to clinical hypnosis contributing to that success. Right? The hypnotic process begins when the client first calls your office or contacts you electronically. Getting the prospect to feel like they called the right hypnotist is paramount and explaining that you use stories to help resolve issues just may differentiate you, although do not mention Aesop up front. But, then again ... nothing wrong with calling yourself an Aesopian hypnotist!

It's important to realize, whether you approach hypnosis as a mind state or an action, there are many solutions. The 'one size fits all' approach is not an effective strategy in truly helping the client, if the role of the professional is to meet the client where they are, as Milton would advocate and, in fact, practice.

The walking path provides a 'platform' that helps the client generate success autonomously from within, creating the resource states they need to make progress. When they can do this, you know you have helped them get on the right path in the present, with confidence and hope for the future they envision. The fable or any hypnotic story they can tell themselves, or hear, serves as a catalyst and can be explored post-session and may, as this book already mentions, assist in achieving a breakthrough and assigning a meaningful value.

And, as you might imagine, while walking that metaphorical welcoming path, a client may experience self-doubt. Anticipate this and prepare them. Teach them how to access that confidence and belief in themselves and in their goals – the very reason they are focused on the goal itself. In my pre-talk I discuss trance, trance utilization and trance in motion and how movement can induce a relaxing and contemplative trance state.

Here are seven 'trance in motion' strategies that I suggest, as tools to reset and rejuvenate:

1. Bilateral Stimulation: putting your whole brain to work through left/right movements.
2. 3,2,1 Anti-anxiety Breath: stimulating the relaxation response while taking back control.
3. Qigong/Tai Chi: Using the slow movements, connecting mind and body to find balance and peace.
4. EMRT: Kevin Martin's 'infinity loop' for stimulating the optic nerve and resolving conflict.
5. Quantum Focusing: a light-hearted focusing system created by Michael Ellner and Alan Barsky.
6. Anchoring: Connecting a calm feeling to an auditory, kinesthetic or visual trigger.
7. Emptying the Rucksack: my own metaphor for easing the burden of carrying a bag of rocks!

I mention them because they are, indeed, important for you to investigate. More will be said in blog posts at www.magicofaesop.com but I do not want to veer too far afield.

Standing Between Earth and Sky

"The best doctor concentrates on prevention instead of fixing disease."

- Nei Jing (475-221 B.C.E.)

I am always amazed at the people I meet along my own welcoming path, knowingly or otherwise. Sometimes people cross our path to deliver a message, others stay with us for the journey and a few are with us for the duration. Decades ago, a colleague-turned-friend, Susan Bellows, sat me down to explain the whole mind-body-spirit interconnection, long before I decided to switch careers. She also introduced me to Chinese medicine and Qigong Grand Master Nan Lu.

This simple Qigong posture of standing between earth and sky is, I am told, one of the best ways to build your chi, especially for the lungs. It's like Tai Chi but standing still.

Google *Nan Lu and the Dragon's Way*. The YouTube video you will find will demonstrate it. I suggest you explore Qigong both as a metaphor and as a very powerful energy building practice for inspiring your clients to access their healing power. You may think it a stretch (pun intended) but, yes, imagine the power of Qigong on the welcoming path (your clients will remember it months and years later), and combining it with the lessons they extract from the fables you share or urge them to discover. Not into the earth and sky pose? Encourage Qigong breathing to calm any anxiety!

Qi (chee), the energy or life force within you and all around you. It is all energy; *everything* is energy. We are all connected. We know this now from discoveries in modern physics. After all, when you break solid matter down into smaller and smaller portions, there is nothing solid or physical about it at all—it is just invisible energy. So, the basic 'building block' of everything in nature and the universe, including our own bodies, is energy.

Essentially, you stand naturally with feet apart, knees slightly bent. Bring arms out in front of you as you gaze forward, standing still, with hands hanging loosely as you take calm relaxing breaths. Hold that pose, breathe, and relax. Allow you to be that connection between the heavens and with mother nature. Go find the video. Teach this to your clients. They will be impressed as rapport builds.

Pro Tip: Investigate Qigong for yourself and your clients, both as a metaphor and, as the exercises are beneficial, and the principles apply! Learn Qigong breathing. The form for 'lifting the sky', which is the first exercise in a famous Qigong set called 18 Luan Hands, is touted as the best and is easiest to learn (they are all easy). Yes, channel Aesop as you are doing them if you would like! As in any meditative experience just allow what surfaces to arrive while you observe without judgement and allow your mind and heart to embrace the wisdom that is revealed. Chapter Questions:

1. We all feel better when we actually know that we are on the right path. What do you think of the welcoming path metaphor?
2. Clients are reassured when they know you are there with them, helping them find courage and confidence. Can you see yourself, in a client session or even between sessions, walking that path with them?
3. We all face obstacles as we try to embrace what life brings us each day. Many if not most are self-created. Can you see yourself coaching the client, as you provide tools to help them go over, under, around or through any obstacle on their path toward their goal or toward happiness in general?
4. Have you tried the Dr. Lu form, standing between earth and sky? Why not take a moment now, before starting the next chapter? It only takes 5 minutes or so. Go find it on YouTube.

Chapter Four:
Feelings. Nothing but Feelings ... and Desires!

Let's shift gears slightly as we stay with feelings.

> *"They may forget what you said, but they will*
> *never forget how you made them feel."*
> - Carl W. Buechner

In the end, it is all about feelings and desires, right? Even if the desire is to have no desires - a subject for another day. Emotional intelligence and self-control are the keys, as you take this advice and begin setting sail toward a new destiny:

> Lao Tzu says it well ... *"Heed your thoughts; they become your words. Heed your words; they become your actions. Heed your actions; they become your habits. Heed your habits, they become your character. Heed your character, it becomes your destiny."*

We become what we think about.

Ironically, Lao Tzu, the author of the Tao Te Ching, lived at the same time as Aesop, thousands of miles apart. Scholars have loosely mapped many of the morals of Aesop's Fables to the lessons of the Tao Te Ching. Over the centuries, from then and earlier to now, cultures handed down wisdom in the form of short stories and parables. No accident, I suppose, that Jesus told many parables to the flock.

Remember that our thoughts lead to beliefs and feelings, and actions which may become, with intention, new behaviors (as LZ just said above). Most of the time they occur automatically, triggered by our subconscious programming over the course of our life. And many times, driven by our intentions to explore our behaviors and consciously involve ourselves in creating new neural network connections that cause the shift we seek!

Briefly, while on the topic of mapping the morals of fables to the work of others, Stoic philosopher and author of *Enchiridion* and *Discourses,* Epictetus (another Phrygian, like Aesop, but who lived from 50-135 AD) is credited with these familiar seemingly Aesopian fable-like sayings:

- *Men are disturbed not by things, but by the view which they take of them.*
- *We have two ears and one mouth so that we can listen twice as much as we speak.*
- *It's not what happens to you, but how you react to it that matters.*
- *No man is free who is not master of himself...*
- *There is only one way to happiness and that is to cease worrying about things which are beyond the power of our will.*

- *First say to yourself what you would be; and then do what you have to do.*
- *Only the educated are free.*
- *Wealth consists not in having great possessions, but in having few wants.*
- *It is impossible for a man to learn what he thinks he already knows.*
- *If you want to improve, be content to be thought foolish and stupid.*

I wonder, as you become more Aesopian in the stories you share with clients, whether you will see some common themes in the morals of Aesop's Fables and Lao Tzu's work, and the work of Epictetus and others. You are on a great journey if that's what you desire! A true renaissance fabulist.

In our work as change agents and facilitators, helping clients find the inner empowerment they need in order to make progress, we know that no change can take place until change takes place. In other words, the client needs to want the change and is willing to make change happen incrementally or all at once. They need to feel the feeling of the change already happening or having taken place!

So that you have the right context for using the magical fables of Aesop, I want to point you to two important bodies of work; Carl Jung's *Archetypes* – which I will only mention here for the reader to explore elsewhere, potentially mapping fable morals with archetypes, and Steven Reiss's work in researching basic human desires and what makes us tick, and which I do explore here now.

As a marketing consultant and copywriter, in my previous career, I used his sixteen core desires (as well as Robert Cialdini's Influence strategies, which you should use in your practice) in my direct marketing work, as explained in my earlier book *How to Generate All the Business You Can Handle,* available on Kindle.

From his research, came the Reiss Motivation Profile, after his passing. As the RMP founder's web site states:

"For (the late) Steven Reiss, there was a mystery in life that he wanted to solve: Why are people the way they are and how do I understand AND predict their behavior?

Using these two questions, he developed the Reiss Motivation Profile, a tool that reveals a person's fundamental goals and values. The personality profile that was created through this has so far helped countless people to understand themselves and other people better. He reduced the main psychological motivators down to 16 basic desires. Assessing each of these 16 motivators in life helps you to create a picture of your intrinsic behavioral motivators, i.e. the things within you that drive you.

This means that every person who receives their results of the Reiss Motivation Profile can see why they consider certain actions to be reasonable; by combining their own, personal, individual motivators in life, they can understand and see the reasons behind their behavior."

I do not hold myself out as a psychologist of any sort, but I do believe that all professional hypnotists ought to have a basic grounding in what motivates people, how habits are formed and how they are changed, first in the mind - all in their professional quest to help clients connect with their authentic self and what they may really seek on a deeper level. The web site further states:

Until now, psychologists have worked on the basis of only a few different, yet dominant, impulses that determine people's actions;

Steven Reiss' empirical research, on the other hand, identified a significant number of factors.

Sigmund Freud believed that libido was almost the only driving force. Alfred Adler believed that people want to belong and become better/grow/learn/be significant/respected and muster the courage to compensate for their flaws. The American psychologist Abraham Maslow considered the striving for self-actualization to be the driver for human behavior.

"These schemata do not take any account of how different people are," says Reiss. There was no system that included human diversity when it came to looking at the motivators for behavior.

What makes people tick is so varied that it cannot be explained by just a few impulses.

In a series of nine, large trials that included over 8000 men and women, Reiss investigated the psychological 'essential motivators', which he later called 'basic desires', that ultimately drive people.

The basic desires that Steven Reiss identified are the result of this comprehensive scientific research. "For the first time in scientific studies, we looked at the question of what motivates individual people," says Reiss. The result is a breakthrough in motivation research, as it enables you to describe precisely what drives people, i.e. their individual needs and motivations behind their actions. "The intensity of individual desires varies widely from person to person," explains the psychologist. "This is what constitutes a personality." Every person has their own, almost unique set of basic desires. Having your individual needs fulfilled makes you happy and content.

You can dive deeper by searching for 'The Reiss Motivation Profile'. For our purposes, I simply want you to be aware of the core desires that your client may reveal (if he or she knows), and how you might map an appropriate fable to help them in their clinical hypnosis journey.

Per what we learn at Changingminds.org, "Steven Reiss has identified sixteen needs based on studies of over 6000 people. Each of these is discussed below. Reiss also developed a 'Profile of Human Needs' as a form of personality instrument, in which people answer a questionnaire that determines the degree of need they have in each dimension, relative to other people. Realizing these can be used to help explain much interpersonal misunderstanding."

Smart marketers know how to appeal to these sixteen core desires. It's time for professional hypnotists or anyone, including sales professionals, who want to be a persuasive and effective communicator.

Here is a brief discussion of each dimension, as explained at their website:

Acceptance

This is the need for social approval by others, to be accepted into society and social groups. Acceptance is related to Maslow's need for belonging. This is important in evolutionary terms as when we are accepted we gain the protection and support of the group. When we are accepted, we can also seek to satisfy other needs, such as starting a family and gaining status.

Curiosity

Curiosity is the drive that pushes us to learn new things. This is important to get us out of our comfort zones and may be considered a fundamental force of evolution. If we did not learn, we would not be able to cope with changing conditions and would soon die out.

Eating

We of course need to eat to survive, which means nature has given us a desire to eat and made it pleasant for us. When we are hungry, we seek food, and the hungrier we are, the greater the urge to eat. We also like to eat 'good food' with pleasant appearance, taste and texture. Even people who have little, when they get more money, they tend to buy nicer food rather than just more cheap food.

Eating marks out the day and helps build circadian rhythms. We also eat socially, and family meals are important events, as are business lunches and romantic dinners.

Family

When asked what is most important to them, many would say their family. We seek to help our families and 'kin selection' is a common principle when making choices. We are also of course driven to build families, which is one reason sex is so pleasurable for us, as is the thrill of love and romance.

Honor

Our personal integrity and a sense of honor is important as we seek consistency between our actions and our values. When a person is consistent then others can predict their actions, which makes them more socially acceptable. While we feel a sense of honor, it is created through the respect that others give us and is related to Maslow's esteem. The rules of honor are often defined by groups and societies and include rules for everyday behavior and also what must be done when the honor of the group or individual is challenged. There may be a need to defend one's honor when one's status or integrity is threatened, which can lead to strange aggressions even where the aggressor will very likely be defeated. Honor cultures are common in regions where there is little rule of law and people live by their reputations.

Idealism

Idealism is an adherence to ideas that are often clean and untainted by the messiness of everyday life. Believing in the ideal makes life easier and may allow us to deny or ignore life's complications. It also helps when the ideal is shared, such as in religions and politics as this helps social cohesion. Idealism can also help with giving one's life greater meaning. Idealism includes the need for fairness and justice, where each person gets what they deserve and those who transgress rules are proportionately punished.

Independence

While we like to belong to groups, we also seek an independence where we feel as a separate person, with our own individuality. Independence helps create our unique sense of identity. Being independent also means not having to obey others all the time and hence also boosts our sense of control.

Order

When there is order, things are predictable, which gives us a sense of control. People who seek order will be more organized and tidier and will plan for an ordered future. This is in contrast with those who leave things to the last minute and are happy with chaos in their lives (these people get their sense of control more from the choices they feel they still have).

Physical activity

Physical activity makes use of our bodies and so creates physical arousal. Physicality is a primitive thing that animals delight in as can be seen as young and adults wrestle and play-fight. In humans we replicate this in physical games such as football and athletic sports.

Power

There are many forms of power, which may be defined as having the potential to achieve our goals, even if others oppose us. Power helps give us a sense of control. It also confers status and lets us move up social hierarchies. It also helps our evolutionary need to survive and to attract and keep the best possible mate (as seen by the way power is attractive for many women).

Romance

Romance is a step along the path to family and replicating our genes. We get a buzz from the excitement of the chase and the thrill of newness and possibility. Love is a powerful force, especially new love, and we can even 'fall in love with falling in love' in a kind of addiction to new romances that never lead to stable relationships.

Saving

One of the curious facts of human motivation is that we gain pleasure in collecting things. This is related to the desire to possess and also can give us an ongoing interest in learning about the collected subject and looking out for items not in our collection. Perhaps an evolutionary driver of this is the need to gather food and things to help our ancestors survive the long cold winters.

Social contact

We like to meet and be with others. Without human contact we become lonely and depressed, which is perhaps why solitary confinement is such a cruel punishment. Contact is sustained and pleasure deepened when we make and meet with friends, who help sustain this need.

Social status

Once we have friends and belong to groups, we seek the esteem of others that will help us gain status. This can be a powerful underlying force and can be seen in many conversations where we duel for supremacy, boasting of our achievements and downplaying those of others.

Tranquility

As well as arousal and action, we like to find peace and quiet. There is much to be said for taking time out to sit and chill, maybe reading a book or just contemplating the stars. Epicurus highlighted this as katastemic happiness, the pleasure of being rather than doing.

Vengeance

In the same manner as the needs for honor and fairness, when we are wronged we seek revenge, typically looking for some form of justice that gives us satisfaction and punishes

*those who transgress against us. We also like to compete,
which is perhaps a structured form of this need.*

Again, I include them here to simply call attention to the fact that, as we help our clients, and we ask, "so what is it you want for yourself?" they may know exactly ... or they may require a little guidance, or even a little self-hypnosis work to arrive at the answer. Most importantly, as you introduce the use of Aesop's fables, you may want to include the sixteen core desires in the selection of your fable along with the moral that you think the client may benefit from hearing. (Don't be surprised if the moral you think is most appropriate is not what may resonate best with the client. Do not assume they take away the same lesson.)

The Fable Plays Two Important Roles

A good friend of mine, Larry Garrett, told me more than once, "I always ask my clients in the hypnosis pre-talk, 'how do you want to feel when you leave my office today and with that new feeling what will be next for you?'" I learned from Larry's comment that this work we do is all about feelings and learning to manage our emotional state as we live each day facing what life brings us. As you might imagine, the morals from Aesop's Fables can be nicely woven into a story that leads to more positive ways to understand, accept and change our feelings, based on our beliefs, and consider our desires. The newfound optimism and courage lead to the right thoughts, the right feelings, the right mental rehearsal and picturing, and the right action for the client.

As you work to understand the current and perhaps deep, long-standing desires of your client, you also need to factor in the emotional state of the client and the trance they are in at the present moment. Of course, trance utilization should be leveraged to help make the desired shift.

Whether you introduce fables to help them with feelings, desired outcomes, or goal progress your clients may be experiencing deep or even recent and sudden feelings in any of these areas, offered as a partial list of possibilities:

• Hurt	• Grief
• Resentment	• Low esteem
• Anger	• Rejection
• Fear	• Inadequate
• Loss	• Relationship pain
• Sadness	• Regret

Making progress along that welcoming path requires a letting go of what needs to go, and an examination of these feelings.

I created a self-hypnosis exercise that anyone can use 'along the journey'. I call it the Snow Globe induction and deepener. Use it to help the client bring forward any of the above, as it relates to what might be in the way of progress. The beauty of it is, in considering the 'content free' hypnosis session, the client need not share a single issue with you and still make tremendous strides. It's all up to them, and your personal style of the change work you facilitate.

The Snow Globe Induction

Imagine holding a snow globe in your hand ... shake it up and imagine seeing all the flakes begin to settle as you place the snow globe on the table in front of you ... and as the flakes do begin to settle ... take a couple of deep breaths ... invite relaxation in ... and as you watch the flakes settle ... and you begin to notice how deep and relaxed your breathing has become ... I wonder if you begin to feel a shift inside ... a person does once in a while and it may be true for you as well ... as the flakes settle, let that be a metaphor for your mind ... your brain waves settling into a nice light hypnotic feeling of inner peace and tranquility ... Imagine the snow globe along a path .... the very path you are walking in life now ... and walking around it ... seeing what you are trying to see ... that you can only see when the flakes settle ... I wonder what you see ... for in the center is YOU ... and your life ... see it from different angles ... quietly observe ... mindfully ... let the center now become the very issue you may be struggling with to resolve ... and just see it ... from all sides ...being open to see it from all angles ... NOW... imagine walking right up to the door on the side of this magical snow globe .... Open it and walk in ... close it behind you now ... and just raise your hand so I know you are there .... Now ... slowly and gently, without disturbing the settled flakes ... walk to the center and find the nice comfortable swivel chair... sit ... get comfortable ... and begin to gaze outward ... as you find that with enhanced clarity you begin to see what you need to see ... obstacles ... successes ... tasks to focus on as you contemplate your intentions ... and what is calling for your attention now ... so now I am going to just be silent for a moment as you swivel and look around ... out at what you see ... and see if there is more to see ... or feel ... or touch ... or smell ... or any of your multisensory sensations ... and now ... begin to simply walk out of the snow globe ... recharged ... rejuvenated ... resilient and refocused ... as you step back onto the welcoming path ... feeling great ... at peace in knowing what you know is all you need to know now ... all else reveals itself as you take small trusting steps each day ... in fact ... knowing that every day in every way you are better and better.

In the context of helping clients to prosper, utilize the fables of Aesop and the metaphor of the welcoming path to remind your clients to focus on what they want, not what they do not want. After all, as wisdom that's been passed down to us, we become what we think about or, in other words, where our attention goes, energy flows. The classic book, As A Man Thinketh, tells us that we tend to get more of what we focus upon. The smoker who wants to stop and is focused on health and breathing free again will do better than the person who simply 'does not want to smoke' any longer. Using my Snow Globe script, which I encourage you to use and share with others, gives the client a quiet and serene respite on their journey toward change.

Finally, now, as we shift back toward the fables once more, the take-aways I would like you to consider adding to your clinical work are:

- Work to understand what is going on in the background so you can be effective in your clinical work, especially in how you will select stories. Uncover the feelings that maybe your client is suppressing, ignoring or otherwise not acknowledging. Feelings which once addressed just may unlock the door to true progress. For example, in working with a weight loss client, after some success and then a plateau, in reviewing the sixteen core desires and in further hypnosis work, I learned about his underlying anger, his long-standing bad marriage, and a general feeling of being underappreciated by his offspring.

- Use the welcoming path as a metaphor for them feeling better about choosing to be on this magical path that is going to, in the words of Emile Coue, "get better and better every day". I always tell them they can rest on their journey and when they find an obstacle, they indeed have the courage to go over it, around it, under it, or through it!

- Teach some basic mindfulness skills in each session so your client is more aware, awakened to the reality of what is, so they can learn to live more hypnotically in the present. As my son wrote in a card to me after my divorce, "the past is gone, the future is not here yet, Dad, so enjoy today". Buddhist priest and author Pema Chodron has a sign with these words in her monastery office! So, teach your clients to *enjoy today.*

- Use your imagination and 'be there' on that welcoming path with your client, on the journey with him or her. Your own visualization of the path will create passion and enthusiasm, and confidence that they can indeed take steps forward and they have more control than they may realize, although, admittedly, some tough choices may lie ahead if they want the change they seek.

The magic is happening. Stay with me as the next chapter will introduce a handful of fables, for reading pleasure, before we go deeper!

Chapter Questions:

1. Can you begin to see yourself using fables in your clinical work? It's okay, if you must, to open up a book of fables or have a fable worksheet you've created and read to them while in hypnosis.
2. How might you use the sixteen core desires to help a client connect with their true goals?
3. Have you read The Miracle of Mindfulness? Will you use the metaphors of washing the dishes or chopping wood to help clients be accountable to do the things they ought?
4. What stories can you share, either from your personal life or 'enlarged' from other client experiences to help your client

find a common ground with you and with other successful clients you've served?

5. Does the metaphor of the welcoming path resonate with you? Can you see yourself using it to introduce the use of fables as stories along the way?

Chapter Five:
Meet Aesop, Phaedrus and Babrius
(And A Few Other Ancient and Modern Fabulists)

Back to the magic of Aesop! Finally!

Let's get in the fable reading mode, both for appreciation and enjoyment.

I have selected a handful of fables that I enjoyed reading in the book by Ben Perry, *Babrius and Phaedrus Fables,* found in the Loeb Classical Library, and translations from Townsend, L'Estrange, de La Fontaine, and others. Of course, these selections have great potential meaning for your clients or anyone with whom you are helping facilitate their desired change.

As I said earlier, Aesop's Fables were never intended for children. They evolved over time to become timeless children's stories, as they were subjected to non-stop rewriting through the years!

This chapter is simply an opportunity to read for personal enjoyment and let your mind play with assigning any meaning or purpose they may hold for you, and perhaps trigger some ways in which you might use Aesopian stories in your practice. Be mindful as you enjoy these selections so as not to allow your subconscious to skip past the story, judge the fable or even dismiss it. These particular selections may have clinical value in your change work efforts. Who knows? I merely introduce them to get your mind into the literary, metaphorical genre known as fables. You'll notice a difference in the story line in those examples where I share more than one translation.

Note, as well, that each fable has a context which set the motivation for its creation. Most of the fabulists, stating with Aesop, spun fables to reflect the issues of the times and the challenges of the citizenry, with a lesson for all.

For example, consider The Frogs Asking for Kings, from Phaedrus's writings:

> When the Athenians were lamenting their sad servitude to Pisistratus the Tyrant, in Athens, (not that he was cruel, but because every burden is grievous to those who are unused to it), and began to complain, Æsop related a Fable to the following effect:

> "The Frogs, roaming at large in their marshy fens, with loud clamour demanded of Jupiter a king, who, by {his} authority, might check their dissolute manners. The Father of the Gods smiled, and gave them a little Log, which, on being thrown {among them} startled the timorous race by the noise and sudden commotion in the bog. When it had lain for some time immersed in the mud, one {of them} by chance silently lifted his head above the water, and having

taken a peep at the king, called up all the rest. Having got the better of their fears, vying with each other, they swim towards him, and the insolent mob leap upon the Log. After defiling it with every kind of insult, they sent to Jupiter, requesting another king, because the one that had been given them was useless. Upon this, he sent them a Water Snake, ho with his sharp teeth began to gobble them up one after another. Helpless they strive in vain to escape death; terror deprives them of voice. By stealth, therefore, they send through Mercury a request to Jupiter, to succour them in their distress.

Then said the God in reply: 'Since you would not be content with your good fortune, continue to endure your bad fortune.'"

"Do you also, O fellow-citizens," said Aesop, "submit to the present evil, lest a greater one befall you."

From Perry's book on Babrius and Phaedrus:

"Babrius is the reputed author of a collection (discovered in the 19th century) of more than 125 fables based on those called Aesop's, in Greek verse. He may have been a hellenized Roman living in Asia Minor during the late 1st century of our era. The fables are all in one meter and in very good style, humorous and pointed. Some are original.

Phaedrus, born in Macedonia, flourished in the early half of the 1st century of our era. Apparently, a slave set free by the emperor Augustus, he lived in Italy and began to write Aesopian fables. When he offended Sejanus, a powerful official of the emperor Tiberius, he was punished but not silenced. The fables, in five books, are in lively terse and simple Latin verse not lacking in dignity. They not only amuse and teach but also satirize social and political life in Rome."

From Phaedrus, who liked to put the fables to verse, as did others who followed:

What from the founder Esop fell,

In neat familiar verse I tell:

Twofold's the genius of the page,

To make you smile and make you sage.

But if the critics we displease,

By wrangling brutes and talking trees,

Let them remember, ere they blame,

We're working neither sin nor shame;

'Tis but a play to form the youth

By fiction, in the cause of truth.

So, presented without commentary, I invite you to enjoy these selections merely for enjoyment. (The next chapter will present fables as I have used them in the office)

The Eagle and the Fox (Perry 1, Gibbs 155)

The eagle befriended the fox but he later devoured the fox's pups. Since she had no power over the eagle, the fox prayed to the gods for justice. Then one day when a sacrifice was burning upon an altar, the eagle flew down and grabbed the sizzling meat to carry it off to his chicks. The meat was so hot that as soon as the chicks ate it, they died.

This fable shows that even if the victims of powerful and wicked people cannot get revenge directly, the gods will nevertheless inflict a punishment on them in response to their victims' prayers.

* * * * * *

The Eagle and the Fox (Caxton 1484)

How the puyssaunt & myghty must doubte the feble Esope reherceth to vs suche a fable / Ther was an Egle whiche came ther as yong foxes were / and took awey one of them / and gaf hit to his yonge egles to fede them with The foxe wente after hym & praid hym to restore and gyue hym ageyne his yong foxe / And the Egle sayd that he wold not / For he was ouer hym lord and maister / And thenne the foxe fulle of shrewdnes and of malyce beganne to put to gyder grete habondaunce of strawe round aboute the tree / where vpon the egle and his yonge were in theyr nest / and kyndeled it with fyre / And whan the smoke and the flambe began to ryse vpward / the Egle ferdfulle and doubtyng the dethe of her lytylle egles restored ageyne the yonge foxe to his moder.

This fable sheweth vs / how the myghty men oughte not to lette in ony thynge the smale folke / For the lytyll ryght ofte may lette and trouble the grete

* * * * * *

The Eagle and the Fox (Townsend, 1867)

An Eagle and a Fox formed an intimate friendship and decided to live near each other. The Eagle built her nest in the branches of a tall tree, while the Fox crept into the underwood and there produced her young. Not long after they had agreed upon this plan, the Eagle, being in want of provision for her young ones, swooped down while the Fox was out, seized upon one of the little cubs, and feasted

107

herself and her brood. The Fox on her return, discovered what had happened, but was less grieved for the death of her young than for her inability to avenge them. A just retribution, however, quickly fell upon the Eagle. While hovering near an altar, on which some villagers were sacrificing a goat, she suddenly seized a piece of the flesh, and carried it, along with a burning cinder, to her nest. A strong breeze soon fanned the spark into a flame, and the eaglets, as yet unfledged and helpless, were roasted in their nest and dropped down dead at the bottom of the tree. There, in the sight of the Eagle, the Fox gobbled them up.

* * * * * *

The Wolf and the Lamb (Phaedrus, Perry 155, Jacobs 2)

Driven by thirst, a Wolf and a Lamb had come to the same stream; the Wolf stood above, and the Lamb at a distance below. Then, the spoiler, prompted by a ravenous maw, alleged a pretext for a quarrel. "Why," said he, "have you made the water muddy for me {while I am} drinking?" The Fleece-bearer, trembling, {answered}: "Prithee, Wolf, how can I do what you complain of? The water is flowing downwards from you to where I am drinking." The other, disconcerted by the force of truth, {exclaimed}: "Six months ago, you slandered me." "Indeed," answered the Lamb, "I was not born {then}." "By Hercules," said {the Wolf}, "{then 'twas} your father slandered me;" and so, snatching him up, he tore him to pieces, killing him unjustly.

This fable is applicable to those men who, under false pretenses, oppress the innocent.

* * * * * *

The Wolf and the Lamb (Townsend)

Wolf, meeting with a Lamb astray from the fold, resolved not to lay violent hands on him, but to find some plea to justify to the Lamb the Wolf's right to eat him. He thus addressed him: "Sirrah, last year you grossly insulted me." "Indeed," bleated the Lamb in a mournful tone of voice, "I was not then born." Then said the Wolf, "You feed in my pasture." "No, good sir," replied the Lamb, "I have not yet tasted grass." Again, said the Wolf, "You drink of my well." "No," exclaimed the Lamb, "I never yet drank water, for as yet my mother's milk is both food and drink to me." Upon which the Wolf seized him and ate him up, saying, "Well! I won't remain supperless, even though you refute every one of my imputations."

The tyrant will always find a pretext for his tyranny.

* * * * * *

The Wolf and the Lamb (Phaedrus, Chris Smart translation)

By thirst incited; to the brook

The Wolf and Lamb themselves betook.

The Wolf high up the current drank,

The Lamb far lower down the bank.

Then, bent his ravenous maw to cram,

The Wolf took umbrage at the Lamb.

"How dare you trouble all the flood,

And mingle my good drink with mud?"

"Sir," says the Lambkin, sore afraid,

"How should I act, as you upbraid?

The thing you mention cannot be,

The stream descends from you to me."

Abash'd by facts, says he, "I know

'Tis now exact six months ago

You strove my honest fame to blot"-

"Six months ago, sir, I was not."

"Then 'twas th' old ram thy sire," he cried,

And so he tore him, till he died.

To those this fable I address

Who are determined to oppress,

And trump up any false pretense,

But they will injure innocence.

The Peacock's Complaint (Perry 509)

A peacock was very unhappy with his ugly voice, and he spent most of his days complaining about it.

"It is true that you cannot sing," said the fox, "But look how beautiful you are!"

"Oh, but what good is all this beauty," moaned the dishearten bird, "with such an unpleasant voice!"

"Oh hear," said the fox, "Each one has its special gift. You have such beauty, the nightingale has his song, the owl has his eyes, and the eagle his strength. Even if you had an eloquent voice, you would still complain about another thing."

Do not envy the gifts of others. Make the most of your own.

* * * * * *

The Peacock and Juno (L'Estrange)

The peacock, they say, lay'd it extremely to heart, that being Juno's darling-bird, he had not the nightingale's voice superadded to the beauty of his own plumes. Upon this subject he petition'd his patroness, who gave him for answer, that Providence had assign'd every bird its proportion, and so bad him content himself with his lot. Moral: The bounties of heaven are in such manner distributed, that every living creature has its share; besides, that to desire things against nature, is effectually to blame the very author of nature itself.

* * * * * *

The Peacock and Juno (Townsend)

The peacock made complaint to Juno that, while the nightingale pleased every ear with his song, he himself no sooner opened his mouth than he became a laughingstock to all who heard him. The Goddess, to console him, said, "But you far excel in beauty and in size. The splendor of the emerald shines in your neck and you unfold a tail gorgeous with painted plumage." "But for what purpose have I," said the bird, "this dumb beauty so long as I am surpassed in song?' "The lot of each," replied Juno, "has been assigned by the will of the Fates–to thee, beauty; to the eagle, strength; to the nightingale, song; to the raven, favorable, and to the crow, unfavorable auguries. These are all contented with the endowments allotted to them."

* * * * * *

The Peacock and Juno (Croxall)

The Peacock presented a memorial to Juno, importing, how hardly he thought he was used, in not having so good a voice as the Nightingale: how that pretty animal was agreeable to every ear that:

111

heard it, while he was laughed at for his ugly screaming noise, if he did but open his mouth. The Goddess, concerned at the uneasiness of her favourite bird, answered him very kindly to this purpose: If the Nightingale is blest with a fine voice, you have the advantage in point of beauty and largeness of person. Ah! says he, but what avails my silent unmeaning beauty, when I am so far excelled in voice! The Goddess dismissed him, bidding him consider, that the properties of every creature were appointed by the decree of fate; to him beauty; strength to the Eagle; to the Nightingale a voice of melody; the faculty of speech to the Parrot; and to the Dove innocence. That each of these was contented with his own peculiar quality: and, unless he had a mind to be miserable, he must learn to be so too.

* * * * * *

The Fox and The Grapes (Croxall, Perry #015)

A Fox, very hungry, chanced to come into a vineyard, where there hung branches of charming ripe Grapes: but nailed up to a trellis so high, that he leaped till he quite tired himself, without being able to reach one of them. At last, let who will take them! says he; they are but green and sour; so I'll even let them alone.

* * * * * *

The Fox and The Grapes (Townsend)

A famished fox saw some clusters of ripe black grapes hanging from a trellised vine. She resorted to all her tricks to get at them, but wearied herself in vain, for she could not reach them. At last she turned away, hiding her disappointment and saying: "The Grapes are sour, and not ripe as I thought."

* * * * * *

112

The Fox and the Grapes (L'Estrange)

There was a time, when a fox would have ventur'd as far for a bunch of grapes as for a shoulder of mutton, and it was a fox of those days, and of that palate, that stood gaping under a vine, and licking his lips at a most delicious cluster of grapes that he had spy'd out there; he fetched a hundred and a hundred leaps at it, 'till at last, when he was as weary as a dog, and found that there was no good to be done; Hang 'em (says he) they are as sowr as crabs; and so away he went, turning off the disappointment with a jest.

* * * * * *

The Fox and the Grapes (JBR Collection)

A hungry Fox one day saw some tempting Grapes hanging at a good height from the ground. He made many attempts to reach them, but all in vain. Tired out by his failures, he walked off grumbling to himself, "Nasty sour things, I know you are, and not at all fit for a gentleman's eating." It is easy to despise what you cannot get.

* * * * * *

The Fox and the Grapes (V. Jones)

A hungry fox saw some fine bunches of grapes hanging from a vine that was trained along a high trellis and did his best to reach them by jumping as high as he could into the air. But it was all in vain, for they were just out of reach. So, he gave up trying and walked away with an air of dignity and unconcern, remarking, "I thought those grapes were ripe, but I see now they are quite sour."

* * * * * *

The Country Mouse and the City Mouse (Perry 352, Gibbs 408)

A city mouse once happened to pay a visit to the house of a country mouse where he was served a humble meal of acorns. The city mouse finished his business in the country and by means of insistent invitations he persuaded the country mouse to come pay him a visit. The city mouse then brought the country mouse into a room that was overflowing with food. As they were feasting on various delicacies, a butler opened the door. The city mouse quickly concealed himself in a familiar mouse hole, but the poor country mouse was not acquainted with the house and frantically scurried around the floorboards, frightened out of his wits. When the butler had taken what he needed, he closed the door behind him. The city mouse then urged the country mouse to sit back down to dinner. The country mouse refused and said, 'How could I possibly do that? Oh, how scared I am! Do you think that the man is going to come back?' This was all that the terrified mouse was able to say. The city mouse insisted, 'My dear fellow, you could never find such delicious food as this anywhere else in the world.' 'Acorns are enough for me,' the country mouse maintained, 'so long as I am secure in my freedom!'

It is better to live in self-sufficient poverty than to be tormented by the worries of wealth.

* * * * * *

The Country Mouse and the Town Mouse (Townsend 216, Perry 352)

A COUNTRY MOUSE invited a Town Mouse, an intimate friend, to pay him a visit and partake of his country fare. As they were on the bare plow lands, eating there wheat-stocks and roots pulled up from the hedgerow, the Town Mouse said to his friend, 'You live here the life of the ants, while in my house is the horn of plenty. I am surrounded by every luxury, and if you will come with me, as I wish you would, you shall have an ample share of my dainties.' The Country Mouse was easily persuaded and returned to town with his friend. On his arrival, the Town Mouse placed before him bread, barley, beans, dried figs, honey, raisins, and, last of all, brought a dainty piece of cheese from a basket. The Country Mouse, being much delighted at the sight of such good cheer, expressed his satisfaction in warm terms and lamented his own hard fate. Just as they were beginning to eat, someone opened the door, and they both ran off squeaking, as fast as they could, to a hole so narrow that two could only find room in it by squeezing. They had scarcely begun their repast again when someone else entered to take something out of a cupboard, whereupon the two Mice, more frightened than before, ran away and hid themselves. At last the Country Mouse, almost famished, said to his friend: 'Although you have prepared for me so dainty a feast, I must leave you to enjoy it by yourself. It is surrounded by too many dangers to please me. I prefer my bare plow lands and roots from the hedgerow, where I can live in safety, and without fear.'

* * * * * *

The Lion and the Mouse (Samuel Croxall)

A Lion, faint with heat, and weary with hunting was laid down to take his repose under the spreading boughs of a thick shady oak. It happened that, while he slept, a company of scrambling Mice ran over his back, and waked him. Upon which, starting up, he clapped his paw upon one of them, and was just going to put it to death, when the little suppliant implored his mercy in a very moving manner, begging him not to stain his noble character with the blood of so despicable and small a beast. The Lion, considering the matter, thought proper to do as he was desired, and immediately released his little trembling prisoner. Not long after, traversing the forest in pursuit of his prey, he chanced to run into the toils of the hunters; from whence, not able to disengage himself, he set up a most hideous and loud roar, The Mouse, hearing the voice, and knowing it to be the Lion's, immediately repaired to the place, and bid him fear nothing, for that he was his friend. Then straight he fell to work, and, with his little sharp teeth, gnawing asunder the knots and fastenings of the toils, set the royal brute at liberty.

* * * * * *

The Lion and the Mouse (Perry 150)

Some field-mice were playing in the woods where a lion was sleeping when one of the mice accidentally ran over the lion. The lion woke up and immediately grabbed the wretched little mouse with his paw. The mouse begged for mercy, since he had not meant to do the lion any harm. The lion decided that to kill such a tiny creature would be a cause for reproach rather than glory, so he forgave the mouse and let him go. A few days later, the lion fell into a pit and was trapped. He started to roar, and when the mouse heard him, he came running. Recognizing the lion in the trap, the mouse said to him, 'I have not forgotten the kindness that you showed me!' The mouse then began to gnaw at the cords binding the lion, cutting through the strands and undoing the clever ingenuity of the hunter's art. The mouse was thus able to restore the lion to the woods, setting him free from his captivity.

Let no one dare to harm even the smallest among us.

* * * * * *

The Lion and the Mouse (Jacobs 11)

Once when a Lion was asleep a little Mouse began running up and down upon him; this soon wakened the Lion, who placed his huge

116

paw upon him, and opened his big jaws to swallow him. "Pardon, O King," cried the little Mouse: "forgive me this time, I shall never forget it: who knows but what I may be able to do you a turn some of these days?" The Lion was so tickled at the idea of the Mouse being able to help him, that he lifted up his paw and let him go. Sometime after the Lion was caught in a trap, and the hunters who desired to carry him alive to the King, tied him to a tree while they went in search of a waggon to carry him on. Just then the little Mouse happened to pass by, and seeing the sad plight in which the Lion was, went up to him and soon gnawed away the ropes that bound the King of the Beasts. "Was I not right?" said the little Mouse.

Little friends may prove great friends.

* * * * * *

The Fox and the Raven (Perry 124, Gibbs 104)

A story about a fox and a raven which urges us not to trust anyone who is trying to deceive us.

The raven seized a piece of cheese and carried his spoils up to his perch high in a tree. A fox came up and walked in circles around the raven, planning a trick. 'What is this?' cried the fox. 'O raven, the elegant proportions of your body are remarkable, and you have a complexion that is worthy of the king of the birds! If only you had a voice to match, then you would be first among the fowl!' The fox said these things to trick the raven and the raven fell for it: he let out a great squawk and dropped his cheese. By thus showing off his voice, the raven let go of his spoils. The fox then grabbed the cheese and said, 'O raven, you do have a voice, but no brains to go with it!'

If you follow your enemies' advice, you will get hurt.

* * * * * *

Robert Martel

Of the Rauen and of the Foxe (Caxton 1484, Perry 124)

They that be glad and loyefull of the praysynge of flaterers oftyme repente them therof / wherof Esope reherceth to vs suche a fable / A rauen whiche was vpon a tree / and held with his bylle a chese / the whiche chese the fox desyred moche to haue / wherfore the foxe wente and preysed hym by suche wordes as folowen / O gentyll rauen thow art the fayrest byrd of alle other byrdes / For thy fethers ben so fayr so bryght and so resplendysshynge / and can also so wel synge yf thow haddest the voys clere and small thow sholdest be the moost happy of al other byrdes / And the foole whiche herd the flaterynge wordes of the foxe beganne to open his bylle for to synge / And thenne the chese fylle to the grounde / and the foxe toke and ete hit / and whan the rauen sawe that for his vayn glorye he was deceyued wexed heuy and sorowfull / And repented hym of that he had byleued the foxe /

And this fable techeth vs / how men ought not to be glad ne take reioysshynge in the wordes of caytyf folke / ne also to leue flatery ne vaynglory

* * * * * *

The Fox and the Crow (Jacobs 8, Perry 124)

A Fox once saw a Crow fly off with a piece of cheese in its beak and settle on a branch of a tree. "That's for me, as I am a Fox," said Master Reynard, and he walked up to the foot of the tree. "Good-day, Mistress Crow," he cried. "How well you are looking to-day: how glossy your feathers; how bright your eye. I feel sure your voice must surpass that of other birds, just as your figure does; let me hear but one song from you that I may greet you as the Queen of Birds." The Crow lifted up her head and began to caw her best, but the moment she opened her mouth the piece of cheese fell to the ground, only to be snapped up by Master Fox. "That will do," said he. "That was all I wanted. In exchange for your cheese I will give you a piece of advice for the future. "Do not trust flatterers."

* * * * * *

The Crow and the Pitcher (Perry 390, Gibbs 453)

A thirsty crow noticed a huge jar and saw that at the very bottom there was a little bit of water. For a long time the crow tried to spill the water out so that it would run over the ground and allow her to satisfy her tremendous thirst. After exerting herself for some time in vain, the crow grew frustrated and applied all her cunning with unexpected ingenuity: as she tossed little stones into the jar, the water rose of its own accord until she was able to take a drink.

This fable shows us that thoughtfulness is superior to brute strength, since this is the way that the crow was able to carry her task to its conclusion, one pebble at a time.

* * * * * *

The Crow and the Pitcher (Jacobs 55)

A Crow, half-dead with thirst, came upon a Pitcher which had once been full of water; but when the Crow put its beak into the mouth of the Pitcher he found that only very little water was left in it, and that he could not reach far enough down to get at it. He tried, and he tried, but at last had to give up in despair. Then a thought came to him, and he took a pebble and dropped it into the Pitcher. Then he took another pebble and dropped it into the Pitcher. Then he took another pebble and dropped that into the Pitcher. Then he took another pebble and dropped that into the Pitcher. Then he took another pebble and dropped that into the Pitcher. Then he took another pebble and dropped that into the Pitcher. At last, at last, he saw the water mount up near him, and after casting in a few more pebbles he was able to quench his thirst and save his life.

Little by little does the trick.

* * * * * *

Two Frogs That Wanted Water (Sir Roger L'Estrange 1692, Perry 43)

Upon the drying of a Lake, two Frogs were forc'd to quit, and to seek for Water elsewhere. As they were upon the Search, they discover'd a very deep Well. Come, (says one to t'other) let us e'en go down here, without looking any further. You say well, says her Companion; but what if the Water should fail us here too? How shall we get out again?

The moral: *'Tis good Advice to look before we leap.*

* * * * * *

The Two Frogs at the Well (Gibbs 445, Perry 43)

There were two frogs whose pond had dried up, so they went looking for a new place to live. When they came to a well, one of them thought that they should jump in immediately, but the other one said, 'Wait: what if the water were to dry up here too; how would we be able to get back out again?'

The story teaches us not to approach a situation without thinking about it carefully first.

* * * * * *

The Two Frogs (Townsend 139, Perry 43)

TWO FROGS dwelt in the same pool. When the pool dried up under the summer's heat, they left it and set out together for another home. As they went along they chanced to pass a deep well, amply supplied with water, and when they saw it, one of the Frogs said to the other, 'Let us descend and make our abode in this well: it will furnish us with shelter and food.' The other replied with greater caution, 'But suppose the water should fail us. How can we get out again from so great a depth?' *Do nothing without a regard to the consequences.*

The above fables were shared to offer a taste of the various translations as well as help build an appreciation for the brevity of the fable. Take a moment to reflect on the simplicity of the story, noting your own receptivity to the moral of the fable. Your clients will do the same!

The fables offered in the following chapter represent actual examples of Aesop's Fables used in my client work. As you read these fables and other selections be aware of how each may help your client to open their mind to new solutions to the issues they are facing. Remember, the client assigns the meaning of the (hypnotic) story you weave, with help from Aesop as needed, through the course of your change work.

In the context of your practice and the services you offer, as you become more comfortable with the fable as a literary genre and as a storytelling tool, I'm confident that you will begin to tailor them to suit your client needs.

Now, let's move on to the promise of this book and delve into some fables with proven clinical impact!

In each chapter I will present a version that I enjoy. I hope you like my selections. I invite you to do your own research, however, and find your favorite version at www.read.gov/aesop, or find your favorite version in the online version of *Three Hundred Aesop's Fables*. You may also simply search for the Hare and the Tortoise online by any of the translators I've mentioned thus far. Gutenberg Press is a great source of fables, ancient and modern. I do suggest you find a favorite illustrated book of Aesop's Fables as a gift for your hypnosis clients, and for friends, children and grandchildren. My grandson, Hunter, is known to sit me down to hear him read a fable. He loves the City Mouse and The Country Mouse! Keep in mind, too, that the inner child, even in the adult, enjoys a good story. Why not read this to them as part of your change work to help their subconscious mind begin to connect with their inner wisdom?

Let's move forward to the clinic use of fables, as I use them, and as you may find useful, too! First up is the story about two animals that run a race to prove a point.

Chapter Six:
How a Slow and Steady Turtle
Changed the World

Like the frogs at the well, let's jump right into the clinical hypnotherapy application of the Aesop's most memorable and popular fable. I present three versions of that famous race between a rabbit and a turtle.

The Hare and The Tortoise (Jacobs 68, Perry 226)

> The Hare was once boasting of his speed before the other animals. "I have never yet been beaten," said he, "when I put forth my full speed. I challenge any one here to race with me." The Tortoise said quietly, "I accept your challenge." "That is a good joke," said the Hare; "I could dance round you all the way." "Keep your boasting till you've beaten," answered the Tortoise. "Shall we race?"
>
> So, a course was fixed and a start was made. The Hare darted almost out of sight at once, but soon stopped and, to show

123

his contempt for the Tortoise, lay down to have a nap. The Tortoise plodded on and plodded on, and when the Hare awoke from his nap, he saw the Tortoise just near the winning-post and could not run up in time to save the race. Then said the Tortoise: "Plodding wins the race."

* * * * * *

The Hare and The Tortoise (Gibbs 2002)

The hare laughed at the tortoise's feet but the tortoise declared, 'I will beat you in a race!' The hare replied, 'Those are just words. Race with me, and you'll see! Who will mark out the track and serve as our umpire?' 'The fox,' replied the tortoise, 'since she is honest and highly intelligent.' When the time for the race had been decided upon, the tortoise did not delay, but immediately took off down the race course. The hare, however, lay down to take a nap, confident in the speed of his feet. Then, when the hare eventually made his way to the finish line, he found that the tortoise had already won.

The story shows that many people have good natural abilities which are ruined by idleness; on the other hand, sobriety, zeal and perseverance can prevail over indolence.

* * * * * *

The Hare and the Tortoise (Townsend 18)

A HARE one day ridiculed the short feet and slow pace of the Tortoise, who replied, laughing: 'Though you be swift as the wind, I will beat you in a race.' The Hare, believing her assertion to be simply impossible, assented to the proposal; and they agreed that the Fox should choose the course and fix the goal. On the day appointed for the race the two started together. The Tortoise never for a moment stopped but went on with a slow but steady pace straight to the end of the course. The Hare, lying down by the wayside, fell fast asleep. At last waking up, and moving as fast as he could, he saw the Tortoise had reached the goal, and was comfortably dozing after her fatigue.

Slow but steady wins the race.

Aesop never put his fables to pen, as you know, but even through the oral tradition that was eventually penned by Phaedrus and Babrius, there are certain patterns we can all agree are present. The use of hypnotic language patterns, persuasive speech and a simple, powerful message are all part of the fabric of his works. Aesop's Fables, like any mesmerizing story in the hypnotist's arsenal, are simply tools for accelerating change so that the progress or desired outcome is realized with greater ease and less internal resistance. We use stories to help the client see things from a new point of view, the story itself becoming an autosuggestion.

Although I have used metaphors and hypnotic storytelling in my clinical hypnosis practice for years, I first used Aesop's Fables to help a client stop her sugar addition. She came to me to help her end her habit of drinking twelve cans of soda each day. After her clear resistance to the hypnotic suggests in my work with her, I decided to try a different angle in my use of storytelling. I was determined to help her lower her resistance without my overt efforts. I was starting to think she really did not want the change we had expressed was so important. Here's what I said to her at the end of the third session, as a posthypnotic suggestion:

Okay Martha ... I want to make a suggestion for you ... something that others have embraced and found to be a true breakthrough ... I wonder if you'll have a similar experience ... so ... I have a gift for you ... and a simple homework assignment ... now, I merely want you to allow that childlike mind to step forward so your subconscious will cooperate and you get that alignment ... that resonance ... fair enough? Here's my gift ... an illustrated copy of Aesop's Fables, a children's edition. As others have done in the change work I've done with them ... they found that a fox, a frog, a turtle, a crow, a lion, mouse, and all sorts of animals have delivered the exact message, through the story, that a person needs to hear. NOW ... all I want you to do is book some time to relax and read a few ... and finish them all before calling me back to book your next appointment. But the book is my gift to you. Then I told her ... I am confident that if you do this ... and I do not know which story ... and you need not share with me ... but your mind will find the exact meaning to help you immediately stop drinking soda and find a healthy replacement.

Within a week, Martha had called me to cancel the next appointment and announce that she did not have any desire, urge, craving, or thought for soda, which was a suggestion offered in the first session, but one that met resistance until Aesop came along. Pretty simple. Proof positive that, with an open mind and an attention-grabbing story, the mind will assign the meaning and value, as well as take action. Who knew that Aesop had discovered neuroplasticity way back then?

If you add this one fable alone to your clinical repertoire, change is inevitable. I've used it in many ways to help all sorts of clients. After all, who can argue with "slow and steady wins the race"? Seems too easy. I wonder if you already see new ways to use this fable?

I've also used it in the following areas:

• Sobriety	• Forgiveness	• Grief

• Anxiety	• Goal progress	• Smoking cessation
• Self-Compassion	• Mindfulness skills	• Gratitude
• Habit Change	• Self-hypnosis	• Self-acceptance

Call it baby steps, as the fictional Dr. Leo Marvin named his book in the movie *'What About Bob?'* or call it slow progress walking along the right and welcoming path. Well planned steps yield confidence, courage, self-esteem, and peace of mind as the client takes back control of their life. There is something to be said, something that resonates with everyone about a sure-footed, determined, and deliberate turtle keen on realizing his goal. Mix your metaphor for humor's sake and ask your client to imagine, like Dorothy, walking the yellow brick road. One step in front of the other with confidence. But, the Wizard of Oz will introduce a potential tangent. Let it. Fables can be a jumping-off point, as the frogs at the well, knew all too well.

Let's be clear. This fable telling is really the art of using fiction in therapy, something that should not be a new concept. We tap into the imaginative mind. We connect the story to our present world with an eye on the future we seek to influence by our new thoughts, new actions, and we further pace the feelings of the progress or the end result already having occurred.

When the client is game, I often take the fable much deeper. I get them to step back and look at the fable from afar. Who are the characters? Can they empathize and see the world through the eyes of the characters? Does the lesson make sense? How do the characters feel? What is their role in the lesson of the fable? Protagonist? Victim?

I AM the Tortoise!

Autosuggestion works. Affirmations are very powerful when utilized properly. Now, imagine you (or your client) giving words of encouragement in the form of affirmations to the turtle. Alternatively, if the hare was actually serious about making the effort to finish the race, affirmations could have changed the outcome of the race!

The power of "I AM" is well-proven. When we declare in the present tense, our subconscious mind hears that statement and when aligned with conscious intention, begins to accept the thought and associated feelings, and moves the body in mind in the direction of the intention, making it real in the mind first!

Emile Coue's famous and powerful affirmation is applicable. It's probably in your game plan anyway.

"Every day and in every way, I am better and better!"

"Every day and in every way, I am better and better at putting one foot in front of the other!"

In his excellent book, *The Power of I Am and the Law of Attraction*, RJ Banks lays out the magic behind using I AM affirmations and explains exactly how to use them, with a library of examples. I've used the power of I Am for several years, as such affirmations demonstrate the choices we make in our daily lives. From my point of view, the secret lies in using positive, present-tense self-talk aligned with your intentions to bring the magic to the words. Here are a few examples:

- I am happy
- I am determined
- I am worthy

- I am kind to myself and others
- I am grateful
- I am calm and relaxed, and in control
- I am focused
- I am capable and deserving
- I am on the right path and it feels great
- I am making better choices every day

You get the idea. Just like the turtle reciting these phrases, or any one of them, your client can self-program and make progress with confidence!

Hack This Fable

Let's have a little fun with this. Now, imagine the turtle, having booked a confidence-building session with you prior to the race. From the fable we already know he was confident. The Emile Coue phrase could help him to increase his focus and determination. You see, the turtle set out to prove he could win the race but he also 'ran his own race' with a winning strategy for himself. Finding the courage and confidence to move forward, on the welcoming path, sometimes comes from knowing others have persevered, and if a fictional tortoise can do it, so can your client!

I will often play with the client in the office and make such suggestions, so the client can peak into the fable and, while appreciating the story through the characters' eyes, they can deepen their connection and reinforce the value to themselves. Try it. It cements the assigned meaning.

Shift Perspective: The Finish Line is the Starting Line (Of A New Journey)

So. Let's take this one step further.

What if the finish line in the race between these two characters was not actually the finish line but, rather, a milestone on their journey toward life? What if it was not a race at all but simply that metaphorical journey, marking goal progress along the way, and enjoying certain benefits as a result of accomplishments. In other words, as I will suggest to clients, the finish line is actually the starting line of whatever comes next. And, I always ask, as the goal is nearing completion, "So, what's next for you now that you have accomplished this?"

This is how I use the Hare and the Tortoise to help clients overcome internal resistance and safely examine how Aesop's characters resolve similar issues. Remember, it's not about the race, per se, but about running one's own race, and it's not a race at all. Yes, you must have conviction and determination. Nobody ever won any race or accomplished any goal by procrastinating or dreaming with no action. You must take the steps toward whatever it is you seek!

Pro Tip: Self-talk is so important to a client's well-being. From Lao Tzu - *Do the difficult things while they are easy and do the great things while they are small. A journey of a thousand miles must begin with a single step. Kindness in words creates confidence. Kindness in thinking creates profoundness. Kindness in giving creates love. Nature does not hurry, yet everything is accomplished.*

Now that you are fast becoming an Aesopian hypnotist, you already know there are many versions of every fable. You are probably already wondering exactly how you will introduce Aesop's Fables into your change work. As you build your fables resources beyond what I present in these pages, you'll begin to know when fables are well suited for your clients' progress. You can create individual client worksheets with a single fable yet be careful not to guide the client toward the moral. Print the fable on your letterhead, exclude the moral, and ask them to read it, even if they think they already know it. Plant the seeds of suggestion using language as I have shared in this chapter.

Chapter Questions:

1. How will you introduce the Hare and the Tortoise to your clients?
2. Will you include it in your sessions, with the client in hypnosis?
3. Will you mention the moral in the posthypnotic suggestions given in the first session, if you see the applicability, based on the client's presenting language?

Chapter Seven:
Thar She Blows? Or Does She?

Aesop and those who followed were notorious for setting two against one another to prove a point. Not that we need to challenge our clients, or any listener of our storytelling, but when we try to share any moral of any fable, our minds shut it down. It's been heard before or the critical faculty in our mind is not going to allow 'a children's story' into our subconscious mind. Who would ever believe that a fox, a crow, a tortoise, an eagle, or even the wind and sun can teach us anything?

This fable helps the client to choose a better strategy when what they are currently doing is, in actuality, keeping them stuck. Sometimes a fable like this can cause the reader, who is filled with intention for shifting their mindset, to lower all resistance and simply begin to see the merits of thinking differently. It illustrates that clients do have more power than they realize.

Three versions of this powerful example of gentle persuasion: The North Wind and the Sun (Townsend 232, Perry 46)

THE NORTH WIND and the Sun disputed as to which was the most powerful and agreed that he should be declared the victor who could first strip a wayfaring man of his clothes. The North Wind first tried his power and blew with all his might, but the keener his blasts, the closer the Traveler wrapped his cloak around him, until at last, resigning all hope of victory, the Wind called upon the Sun to see what he could do. The Sun suddenly shone out with all his warmth. The Traveler no sooner felt his genial rays than he took off one garment after another, and at last, fairly overcome with heat, undressed and bathed in a stream that lay in his path.

Persuasion is better than Force. Kindness wins.

* * * * * *

The Wind and the Sun (Samuel Croxall)

A DISPUTE once arose betwixt the North-wind and the Sun, about the superiority of their power; and they agreed to try their strength upon a traveller, which should be able to get his cloak off first. The North-wind began, and blew a very cold blast, accompanied with a sharp. driving shower. But this, and whatever else he could do, instead of making the man quit his cloak, obliged him to gird it about his body as close as possible. Next came the Sun; who breaking out from a thick watery cloud, drove away the cold vapors from the sky, and darted his warm sultry beams upon the head of the poor weather-beaten traveller. The man growing faint with the heat, and unable to endure it any longer, first throws off his heavy cloak, and then flies for protection to the shade of a neighboring grove.

Gentleness and kind persuasion win where force and bluster fail.

* * * * * *

The Wind and the Sun (Jacobs 60, Perry 46)

133

The Wind and the Sun were disputing which was the stronger. Suddenly they saw a traveller coming down the road, and the Sun said: "I see a way to decide our dispute. Whichever of us can cause that traveller to take off his cloak shall be regarded as the stronger. You begin." So, the Sun retired behind a cloud, and the Wind began to blow as hard as it could upon the traveller. But the harder he blew the more closely did the traveller wrap his cloak round him, till at last the Wind had to give up in despair. Then the Sun came out and shone in all his glory upon the traveller, who soon found it too hot to walk with his cloak on.

Kindness effects more than severity. Gentle persuasion is stronger than force.

* * * * * *

Here is one translator's version, cast for children:

The North Wind boasted of great strength. The Sun argued that there was great power in gentleness. "We shall have a contest," said the Sun. Far below, a man traveled a winding road. He was wearing a warm winter coat. "As a test of strength," said the Sun, "Let us see which of us can take the coat off of that man."

"It will be quite simple for me to force him to remove his coat," bragged the Wind.

The Wind blew so hard, the birds clung to the trees. The world was filled with dust and leaves. But the harder the wind blew down the road, the tighter the shivering man clung to his coat. Then, the Sun came out from behind a cloud. Sun warmed the air and the frosty ground. The man on the road unbuttoned his coat. The sun grew slowly brighter and brighter. Soon the man felt so hot, he took off his coat and sat down in a shady spot. "How did you do that?" said the Wind. "It was easy," said the Sun, "I lit the day. Through gentleness I got my way."

Clearly, the north wind was on a hero's journey, until the sun stepped in to show another way forward. More on this later!

We can only imagine the circumstances in which Aesop created this fable to settle a quarrel between two ominous forces of nature. What creativity! Based on his fables told to his master Xandrus and the citizens of Delphi, we might assume it was to teach a Greek philosopher a lesson after the fact. The strength of the winds versus the power and wisdom of the sun. As with all of his fables and the morals found within, using the story to indirectly influence the subconscious mind is more effective than a direct suggestion or overt advice. Again, we see the magic of the story lowering resistance and increasing acceptance.

What I like about this fable in particular is how the metaphor illustrates that we often tend to approach the solution to a problem using only our own devices and then allow our beliefs that other solutions either do not exist or are inferior. For me, one of the lessons I share with clients who do not extract their own meaning so readily, is that sometimes we are so caught up in own apparent superpowers that our ego will not entertain other ideas. Sometimes we just need to think different thoughts.

No motivational quotes are offered here, although tempting, but this change work is all about thinking differently, and deciding that seeing things from a different perspective and perhaps making new choices in alignment with the stated goal is, well, a damn good idea to entertain!

Imagine a different version of this fable:

The sun and the north wind decided to go to the local coffee shop to discuss their thoughts and feelings about the guy wearing the silly coat, standing on the sidewalk. The wind said, "You know, I have four winds, the strongest coming from the north. But before I blow the man down and the coat into the air, how might you get his coat off, Mr. Sun?" They talked all morning about it and the guy in the coat just stood there, as if defying them to try. After a couple of lattes and a toasted garlic and asiago bagel with chive cream cheese, they agreed that the sun could try first. The north wind would save his energy to blow the incoming storm to sea. The sun focused a beam of heat and, voila, the coat came off! The moral? You figure it out!

In my practice, I use this fable for clients who are struggling to give themselves permission to see things differently. I'll use the snow globe induction and deepener presented earlier in the book, or I will ask them to imagine them seeing the picturesque Grand Canyon from different viewpoints; the north wall, from space, from the Colorado River below, or from the tourist visitor's center, perhaps from the mule ride down the canyon walls. A different experience from each angle.

- *I'll combine this with the Frogs that wanted Water fable:*

   "Now, I wonder if you can pause and reflect on your options before jumping on the solution that seems most obvious to you now ... is your current thinking and planned action going to lead to the best possible outcome? ... you may not see other solutions at this moment but your brute force approach just may not bring about what you desire ... with a little self-compassion ... and kindness toward others ... is there a more persuasive alternative ... I wonder if you'll open your mind to that possibility?"

- *I will print this fable and the recast fable I presented above on my office letterhead and make it a reading assignment; without any discussion of the lesson they might assign to the story. It's something to be discussed at the next session. I do offer a posthypnotic suggestion: "You might find this useful reading, as other people have as well. See you next week."*

- *I teach self-hypnosis techniques to every client I serve. It's essential to their continued success far beyond the session work. While I do not introduce Aesop's Fables into every client's change work, when it applies, I always include the Sun and the North Wind.*

- *I also make sure each client receives a little introduction to mindfulness; what it is, how it compares to hypnosis, and why it's so important to be more self-aware. Sometimes we use brute force to get what we think we want, or the hero archetype (which is often needed!) tries to break through to save the day. I've had one client find a stronger connection to God using this fable, inspired by the kindness and compassion presented in the moral. Psalm 36:7 "How excellent is thy lovingkindness, O God! therefore the children of men put their trust under the shadow of thy wings."*

Hypnotize the Wind!

Pretend for a moment that the north wind booked a session with you. He was flummoxed by the sun's success and is feeling rather unheroic! "Let's talk about this hero's journey stuff that everybody keeps telling me to explore," says the north wind. So, being a student of Greek mythology (play along with me, okay?), you decide to help him to see himself differently, as you explain that the four cardinal winds are deities in nature, as is the sun, each with powers that must be respected. You remind him of their progenies, Eos and Astraeus, and his role in the weather! You establish that it's okay to call him Boreas, his Greek name for the cold north wind, with a reputation for being very strong and violent-tempered at times. You tell him about Herodotus, and his writing about Hyperborea, that place "beyond the north wind" where people live in total happiness. You also tell him about his brothers Zephyrus, god of the gentle west winds, Notus, god of the south winds, and Eurus, god of the east winds. Boreas could have opted to consult his brothers before trying in vain to blow the coat off the man in the story. His hero archetype demanded satisfaction!

Carl Jung wrote in Archetypes and the Collective Unconscious:

> "The hero's main feat is to overcome the monster of darkness: it is the long-hoped-for and expected triumph of consciousness over the unconscious."

The world needs more heroes in all walks of life, but sometimes the hero that lies in our unconscious unawareness needs to sit down long enough to take a deep breath and pause before coming to the rescue. In this session with the north wind, I wonder if it makes sense to help the wind to see, in hypnosis, to help him understand the Hero Archetype and connect with his truer purpose. Or, if you are really wanting to explore another culture's stories, consider researching the samurai's journey from Edo to Kyoto in 1868 when, during the Meiji Restoration in Japan, they because Ronan; leaderless warriors looking for a purpose. Ask the north wind to start a journal and write about some of his important triumphs in weather history around the globe. Ask him to write down when he could have been kinder and gentler to the people in the paths of the storms he blew!

An important digression, I would argue, shared only to illustrate the depth at which you might decide to explore the value of using

Aesop's Fables and how the stories can be a jumping-off point. I hardly do it any justice at all, but maybe your client (and perhaps yourself as well) needs to explore the hero's journey. It may be life-changing if you'll only take that step! Make Joseph Campbell proud.

Empathize with Boreas, the north wind, and help him understand his transformational journey. He needs your help now that he was outsmarted by the sun. He's hurting. Tell him the fable found in the next chapter. Help the protagonist to change. Think about it. You being an Aesopian hypnotist using a fable to help a fable character to change, if he is willing to change, and blow a gentler breeze or step aside when others have a better solution. Help him appease the guardians of the gates of change so they will let new ideas pass.

Content-Free Hypnosis

There is a trend in clinical hypnosis work showing in many cases that it is not necessary at all for a client to reveal the details of their conscious and subconscious thought. I shared an example earlier of the client who kicked her sugar habit by using Aesop's Fables to stop drinking Coca Cola.

As Jason Linett says in his Context and Content section of Hypnotic Workers: "As we start to bridge the gap between how to hypnotize and how to produce change, there are some strategies that kind of ride the two. Whether they're deepening techniques, whether they're actual change techniques, though it does enter into this conversation of what could be deemed as content-free hypnosis, which this is what I mean in terms of...I mentioned the whole conversation of imagery...remember, that your dream location is someone else's nightmare. So just because you like going to the beach and walking on the sand doesn't mean your client likes it." Content-free hypnosis techniques are client-centered and call upon their resource states and imagery, with your guidance, instead of your suggestions of imagery which may not resonate. Learn more at

www.worksmarthypnosis.com

I frequently use content-free hypnosis techniques with my clients, especially when I introduce an Aesop's fable: "now ... as you relax deeper ... and as you allow your mind to hear what it needs to hear ... for all of the right reasons ... because this is all so important and because ... you know why you are here ... working to make a shift ... of course, you will decide what to share ... that is not important ... you see, your mind knows what needs to change ...and the right strategies ... and the right stories to make change so effortless ... will begin to emerge ... you will find that inner connection and make change start to happen." With that said, I often have a gift-wrapped copy of Aesop's Fables which I hand to them as they leave my office!

Pro Tip: It's great if the fables I present in this book, as examples of my clinical hypnosis work, work for your clients, too. Of course, you'll build your own library, but you can also reverse engineer the process! Perhaps for the second or third session it becomes apparent that an Aesop's fable can help cause the client's desired shift. Ah, but which fable to use? Now there's the rub! This one is a favorite.

Chapter Questions:

1. Do you remember this fable? What does it mean to you?
2. Can you imagine helping the north wind to ease up a bit and try to be a kinder, more gentle soul?
3. What do you think of content-free hypnosis?
4. What are your thoughts on exploring the hero's journey with Boreas, or with your clients?
5. How will you use this fable?

Chapter Eight:
To Thine Own Self Be True!

It's a memorable line, to be sure. Shakespeare has used this phrase in his play, *Hamlet.* Polonius spoke these words as a token of advice to his son, Laertes, as he left for Paris.

Polonius:

> "This above all: to thine own self be true,
>
> And it must follow, as the night the day,
>
> Thou canst not then be false to any man.
>
> Farewell, my blessing season this in thee!"
>
> (Hamlet, Act-1, Scene-III, 78–82)

Shakespeare is known for using both irony and humor to get his points across in his plays. Much truth is said in jest. Polonius is one of those characters who is not high-minded, yet he speaks as a scholar, creating humor and satire. Supposedly, the speeches by Polonius in this play are Shakespeare's maxims for living a good life, and likely influenced by Aesop. Shakespearean scholars, reconstructing the younger days of the Bard's childhood school days, have documented that the readings of Aesop were a daily classroom activity, thus the proven influence.

Note to reader: Like Aesop and his fable morals, Shakespeare coined numerous phrases presented in his writings as satire and humor, but on a deeper level were lessons for life as well. While it's tempting here to go off on this tangent, I will not! Instead, why not bring a little Shakespearean wit and wisdom into your practice? I post a few familiar observations at the end of this chapter.

Now, back to Aesopian storytelling!

Why are so many people unhappy, unable to sleep, popping anxiety meds or just stuck in a rut, unable to move themselves forward in life? Are they trying to be someone they are not?

I find that living a life of authenticity goes a long way toward finding peace of mind and learning to live in the present moment. This is a popular and very important fable.

The Frog and the Ox (Townsend 77)

An ox drinking at a pool trod on a brood of young frogs and crushed one of them to death. The Mother coming up, and missing one of her sons, inquired of his brothers what had become of him. 'He is dead, dear Mother; for just now a very huge beast with four great feet came to the pool and crushed him to death with his cloven heel.' The Frog, puffing herself out, inquired, 'if the beast was as big as that in size.' 'Cease, Mother, to puff yourself out,' said her son, 'and do not be angry; for you would, I assure you, sooner burst than successfully imitate the hugeness of that monster.'

Do not envy others. Be yourself.

* * * * * *

Robert Martel

The Frog and the Ox (Perry 376)

A poor man perishes when he tries to imitate rich and powerful people.

There was once a frog who noticed an ox standing in the meadow. The frog was seized by a jealous desire to equal the ox in size so she puffed herself up, inflating her wrinkled skin. She then asked her children if she was now bigger than the ox. They said that she was not. Once again, she filled herself full of air, straining even harder than before, and asked her children which of the two of them was bigger. 'The ox is bigger,' said her children. The frog was finally so indignant that she tried even harder to puff herself up, but her body exploded and she fell down dead.

* * * * * *

Of the Oxe / and of the frogge / whiche wold haue compared her to hym (Caxton, 2.2, 1484)

The poure ought not to compare hym self to hym which is ryche and myghty / As sayth this fable of a frogge / whiche was in a medowe / where she aspyed and sawe an oxe whiche pastured / She wold make her self as grete and as myghty as the oxe / and by her grete pryde she beganne to swelle ageynste the oxe / And demaunded of his children yf she was not as grete as the oxe and as myghty / And theyr children ansuerd and sayd nay moder / For to loke and behold on the oxe / it semeth of yow to be nothynge / And thenne the frogge beganne more to swelle / And when the oxe saw her pryde / the tradde and thrested / her with his fote / and brake her bely /

Therfore hit is not good to the poure to compare hym self to the ryche / wherfore men sayn comynly / Swelle not thy self / to thende that thow breste not

* * * * * *

144

The Ox and the Frog (Jacobs)

"Father," said a little Frog, "I have seen such a terrible monster! It was as big as a mountain, with horns on its head, and a long tail, and it had hoofs divided in two." "Tush, child," said the old Frog, "that was only Farmer White's Ox. It isn't so big either; he may be a little bit taller than I, but I could easily make myself quite as broad; just you see." So he blew himself out, and blew himself out, and blew himself out. "Was he as big as that?" asked he. "Oh, much bigger than that," said the young Frog. Again, the old one blew himself out, and asked the young one if the Ox was as big as that. "Bigger, father, bigger," was the reply. So the Frog took a deep breath, and blew and blew and blew, and swelled and swelled and swelled; and said: "I'm sure the Ox is not as big as that." At this moment he burst.

Trying to be someone you are not can get you in trouble. Be happy being yourself.

The moral of the story is open to interpretation, as all are: Be true to yourself and live your own life. Be content with being your authentic self, if you dare to take that inner journey. Be true to your own character. Yes, have goals, but accept yourself and do not try to be someone else. This is so true in life and your clients can assign the right value when they enjoy this fable. Their future peace of mind and happiness greatly depend upon it.

This particular fable resonates with the person struggling to make everyone else happy, placing him or herself lower on the priority list. In clinical work, we often find ourselves helping a client get "unstuck" and many times they are unaware or not facing the reasons they are anxious or not making making forward progress in their lives. How many times have you heard "I just want to be myself again" or "I need to reconnect with myself?" I use this fable (or simply state the moral, or Shakespeare's line at the top if this chapter) to help them reset and take back control of their life. We work on courage and confidence, getting on that 'welcoming path' and taking small steps or bold action to begin to make the visualized change and the future-paced feelings real.

I might say to the client:

"As you relax deeper, I wonder if you are able to enjoy that multisensory experience we talk about in hypnotherapy work... one that allows you to journey down into that place within you... that let's you reconnect with your true self... and explore what is truly important in your life... you may know... or maybe your mind reveals in time... bit by bit... as you are better and better every day... in accessing that vast resource within you... your wisdom and the knowings... the learnings... the experience... and your values... that let you ponder and perhaps restart... reset... rejuvenate... or simply to begin now... in this moment and as you move forward in time and space... I wonder if you can learn from that frog in this fable... the Ox and the Frog... that is it better to live your own life rather than try to imitate or become someone else.

In this fable, believed to be created by Phaedrus, the frog is motivated by envy wanting to be like the ox, and choosing to imitate the powerful creature. In the end, the frog comes to his own end, literally. It's a great metaphor for the client who may need to see the danger signs and the fate the lies ahead when a life of keeping up with the Joneses; people trying to outdo each other in their material pursuits. They get lost in the whole process, often losing sight of what they should be focused on, which is different for everyone but includes, love, happiness, joy and abundance (whatever that means to them). After all, this is what God wants for all of us, thus the commandment; thou shalt not covet.

So, pun, intended, this fable has legs and can be applied to a wide range of client issues. Telling the story, in the form of a short and memorable fable, is so much better than spewing direct advice which may roll off like water on a duck's back.

Indeed, self-deceit leads to self-destruction and is a major distraction in life, which makes happiness elusive. When I have a conversation in a light trance state, fully with the client in helping them make progress, when we can get crystal clear on what they want, and what obstacles are impeding them, the solutions begin to appear. I find that clients all want peace of mind and more happiness. This fable goes a long way toward helping the client see a need to shift their perspective, and their thinking. New thoughts lead to new actions which leads to new behaviors and new habits, ultimately leading to a new and more fulfilling destiny. Use this fable to shift the trajectory of their life!

Chapter Nine:
Four Personal Favorites That Belong in Your Fabulist's Toolbox

You will certainly create your own list. Here are four that I had to include:

The Miser and His Gold

Once upon a time there was a Miser who used to hide his gold at the foot of a small tree in his garden; but every week he used to go and dig it up and gloat over his gains. A robber, who had noticed this, went and dug up the gold and stole it. When the Miser next came to gloat over his treasures, he found nothing but the empty hole. He tore his hair and raised such an outcry that all the neighbors came around him, and he told them how he used to come and visit his gold. "Did you ever take any of it out?" asked one of them.

"Nay," said he, "I only came to look at it."

"Then come again and look at the hole," said a neighbor; "it will do you just as much good."

Wealth unused might as well not exist. Gifts and blessings were given to you to share. There are many who pretend to despise and belittle that which is beyond their reach.

* * * * * *

The Fox and the Tiger

A SKILLFUL ARCHER, coming into the woods, directed his arrows so successfully that he slew many wild beasts, and pursued several others. This put the whole savage kind into a fearful consternation and made them fly to the most retired thickets for refuge. At last, the Tiger resumed courage, and, bidding them not to be afraid, said that he alone would engage the enemy; telling them that they might depend upon his valor and strength to revenge their wrongs.

In the midst of these threats, while he was lashing himself with his tail, and tearing up the ground for anger, an arrow pierced his ribs, and hung by its barbed point in his side. He set up an hideous and loud roar, occasioned by the anguish which he felt, and endeavored to draw out the painful dart with his teeth; when the Fox, approaching him, inquired with an air of surprise who it was that could have strength and courage enough to wound so mighty and valorous a beast! "Ah!" says the Tiger, "I was mistaken in my reckoning: it was that invincible man yonder."

Moral: There is always some vulnerable part in the strongest armor.

* * * * * *

Robert Martel

The Lion and the Mouse

A lion is fast asleep until a mouse wakes him up. The lion opens his big jaw to swallow him. But the mouse begs the lion to think again, as he may become useful in the future. The lion laughs the idea off and lets him go. Sometime later, the lion is caught in a trap by some Hunters. At that moment the same little mouse walks by and notices the lion trapped. He walks up and chews the rope to free the lion. The mouse smiles and says, was I not right?

Little friends may prove great friends. You never know who will prove to be useful in the future. It is best to maintain great relationships with everyone and to be kind to all. You never know where your kindness could lead you! No act of kindness is ever wasted.

* * * * * *

The Hart and the Hunter: Don't Underestimate Yourself!

A Hart is drinking at a river, admiring its beautiful antlers. He then notices how small and weak his legs look. Just then out of nowhere, a Hunter approaches and shoots an arrow. The Hart runs away into the woods and realizes that it was thanks to his legs that he survived. While he is looking at his legs, his antlers get caught in the trees. The Hunter Catches up to the Hart and kills it.

We often despise what is most useful to us. Our greatest weaknesses can also be our strengths. A way of us fitting into the world.

Hey, a short chapter, but four fables I needed to point out! Enjoy adding them to your work!

Chapter Ten:
Aesop, The Servant Leader Storyteller

As we near the end of this book, I want you to keep these two things in mind.

1. You are the keeper of the craft; the art of oral storytelling as it pertains to the profession of clinical hypnotism and in all walks of life. Written stories certainly have their place, but it is the spoken word, the mesmerizing stories you tell that matter most.

2. Facts tell. Stories sell. An old phrase yet so true. It's also true that when the student is ready the teacher appears. You are a teacher and storyteller, guiding the listener on their hero's journey using the craft of oral storytelling, helping them live a more courageous and confident life, taking lessons vicariously through the stories you engineer for their benefit or enjoyment.

Since the premise and the promise of this whole book is centered on transformational change using stories, it's important to note that

151

Aesop's Fables provide a lesson for the business world as well – your business, and the business world of your clients. Hypnotic storytelling is powerful, with or without animal characters delivering the story and the lesson! Yet, if you dare, you can weave a little Aesopian storytelling into your role in your daily work life.

Look at it this way. If the magic of the fables themselves is the lowered resistance to a message, then you can compound your effectiveness – and influence compliance – with a good story! Brevity is key to holding attention. That's why the fables of the brilliant Aesop were so short!

Here's an example:

"You know, Bill, believe it or not ... as I was listening to a friend telling me about his own childhood and ... how much he enjoys reading stories to his kids at bedtime ... something he does almost every night. He was sharing what he described as an out of body experience. He could feel his awareness of what he was doing, like he was across the room, watching himself tell a story to his kid ... he could see all of the details ... he could see the book – Aesop's Fables – and he could see his kid enjoying the time with his dad. Isn't that the perfect gift to give a child? ... time! In the end, that is all that matters ... anyway, I started thinking about you ... and our meeting ... that we are having right now ... and how none of us actually manage time ... we move through it and manage ourselves through time and space ... all given the blessing of the same twenty-four hours ... each day ... one day at a time ... my friend's story got me to thinking about my own time and how I chose to use it ... and the importance of being present with people ... as we are now ... fully present in the moment here together. I started looking at my friend as a hero – not my hero – but the hero in his own personal life with his family ... Who would have expected that a dad reading

Aesop's Fables would make me pause to think about my own life and what's important to me? ...

Anyway, what's important is that we focus on your story ... and what's next? What action is required to move ahead with a decision?"

If you notice, a variety of techniques were used in the above story, all designed to get Bill to focus on what's important and what's next. Regression. Social proof. Future pacing, present moment living, mindfulness. Useful in a clinical hypnosis session, or in a business meeting. This story could even be incorporated into a presentation. Keep in mind, that in telling a good story, the listener as well as the secondary character in the story, desperately want something. (See Steven Reiss's 16 Core Desires in chapter four). In any case, try to depict the listener as the hero in his or her own story. Take them on their own hero's journey.

In the stories you tell your sales prospects, whether you are a hypnotist or a professional salesperson or in any profession really, make sure your story highlights what I call the benefits of the benefits. In talking about other heroes' journeys, accentuating the true, deeper value of the purchase decision is magical.

How Storytelling Affects the Brain

We are hard-wired to respond to the power of storytelling, as you know by now! Whether curling up with a book, mesmerized by a movie, or listening to friends recount their adventures, we are enthralled by a good story. Edward Bernays, the 'father of public relations' and the cousin of Sigmund Freud, discovered and exploited the power of storytelling and started the science of mass media manipulation.

You see, we tend to respond best when information is presented in a good narrative, and Aesop's Fables create that backdrop. Best of all, they are stories ready to go, out of the box, and well-proven over the past 2,500 years or more. Brevity is key, as his short fables attest.

Much has been researched and written on the science of storytelling and its effect on the brain. The fact is stories make information memorable, relatable, and understandable so the message is conveyed. It is the perfect platform in short-form communication!

Here is what is going on:

- Neural Coupling: The science of studying the impact of a good story demonstrates the keys to effective communication. When a listener hears or reads a good story, resonance occurs between the brains of the storyteller and the recipient. Neurons fire in the same patterns; the speaker's brain and the listener's brains are in sync, tuned in to the same message. 'Mirror neurons' create coherence between a speaker's brain and the brains of his/her audience members.

- Dopamine: The brain releases dopamine to help remember an emotionally charged event. It is known as the 'feel good' neurotransmitter, sending signals between neurons. We trigger dopamine when we eat comfort foods, have sex, or even when we hear a good story!

- Cortex Activity: When we process facts, the brain stimulates two areas; Broca and Wernicke. When we connect to a good story, the brain lights up. The sensory cortex, motor cortex, auditory and visual cortex, the olfactory and the cerebellum all wake up!

Storytelling lights up more of the brain than a simple litany of facts and connects the listeners emotionally to the speaker, and to each other. Well-proven. Therefore, it is such a powerful tool in affecting human behavior. Aesop knew that, long before neuroscience came to be, and now you have this insight! Use it!

Emotionally engaging stories can change brain chemistry by producing oxytocin, a substance that is shown to increase trustworthiness, generosity, compassion, and sensitivity to various social cues.

Sometimes a product or service presents its own story, usually found in client testimonials, market acceptance, and brand reputation. Adding the power of storytelling to your efforts – in any setting, makes you a more effective and memorable person.

There is a strong connection between organizational storytelling and effective, authentic leadership in business. The fables of Aesop offer a moral dimension to leader storytelling that can contribute to the transformation of an organization's culture; having a positive impact on feeling connected to a higher purpose, such as the company's mission and values, and role in the larger community. Just like sharing a timely smile, a well-said story of any length.

It must be done with aforethought to be effective. Just telling better stories might have some magical qualities but the true magic, the ultra-magic, comes from telling stories that you design to influence and persuade the listener to take action. The key in telling a good, ethical story in business lies in relating to the listener and creating subconscious resonance. Combining personal experiences, perhaps sharing how others have faced a challenge, and tapping into the imagination to visualize future benefits already realized in the listener's mind.

155

This can be seen in any well-done television advertisement. TED talks demonstrate the power of a well-told story. Better yet, though, is the power of a hypnotic story in both one-to-one and small group communication such as a business meeting. Telling emotionally powered stories help you be unforgettable while also helping you break through all the distractions and noise that prevents focused concentration. Yes, your story has a hypnotic effect on your listeners. It moves them to action, to take next steps in their lives.

As you are reading this right now, you may feel some intimidation about your storytelling skills, or even sense an awareness that you are nervous about the very idea. The fact that you have read this far into this book speaks volumes about your desire to tell actionable and memorable stories, hopefully with the wisdom of Aesop's storytelling abilities. He has laid it all out for you. Structure, design, the words. Ready to go, but ready for your craftsmanship as you deem necessary for your client's progress!

It's now time for you to begin crafting your own story – to telegraph your own values, characters and traits, and to touch the lives of people in a new way. Crafting stories that deepen relationships and build strong rapport are on your horizon.

You have to conceive, believe and achieve your story in your own mind first if you hope for others to believe you. Walking the talk, as they say, or achieving authenticity and congruence of your conscious and subconscious mind as you align with your intentions, which drive everything.

Let's wrap this up!

Chapter Eleven:
Final Words – Aesop Lives!

Aesop lives amongst us in so many ways, far beyond his fables.

He may have been tossed off a cliff in Greece for offending the Delphinians but Aesop lives within us, although dormant it may seem. His teachings, which are proven to have influenced Jesus and the authors of the *Bible,* have universal appeal and adults of all ages carry with them the lessons from the fables that resonate.

His words continue to influence those who were exposed to or studied him further. He inspires us towards our better self, be it by lessons of gratitude or through insightful wisdom that we store in our critical faculty for guidance through life. Aesop's Fables are still taught as moral lessons, primary in the form of children's books today. Adults, too, can enter the realm of Aesop's imagination and either recall or remember for the first time the lessons he imparted.

Considered both humble and thought-provoking with a simple message delivered for one's interpretation and applicability, his fables and the Aesopic traditional fables that stretched from his time 600 years BC to the 13th century were transformational. You could argue, as I have proven to myself in my clinical hypnosis work and I hope you as well may realize, that Aesop's Fables are, indeed, hypnotic. Long before the phenomenon of hypnosis, fables were the style du jour for hypnotic storytelling in that era, reaching way back to the days of the Greek tragedy.

After all, to revisit briefly here, who does not remember these impactful hypnotic suggestions:

- *No act of kindness, no matter how small, is ever wasted.*
- *First, set thyself upright, and then boldly mayest you check other men.*
- *Slow and steady wins the race.*
- *Do not count your chickens before they are hatched.*
- *The gods help them that help themselves.*
- *Put your shoulder to the wheel.*
- *Once a wolf, always the wolf.*
- *Any excuse will serve a tyrant.*
- *What a splendid head, but no brain.*
- *In union there is strength.*
- *Gratitude is the sign of noble souls.*
- *Please all, and you will please none.*
- *It is easy to be brave from a safe distance.*
- *After all is said and done, more is said than done.*
- *Better to be wise by the misfortunes of others than by your own.*

As we wrap up, I recommend that you compile your own index of morals and find the associated fable, as if reengineering the process. Start at www.litscape.com and search for Aesop's morals. They are there for you, as a starting point, selectable by starting line, ending line, moral, etc.

You are well armed now, prepared to help the client find easy, non-resistant ways to bring the lessons of Aesop's Fables and other hypnotic stories into their realm so they can take the right action. You see, like the philosophers of old, we all want to be like Aesop; wise, witty, stoic, calm, charismatic, happy.

It is your turn now

Go forth and be Aesopian and Ericksonian in your change work!

Here are your action steps:

- Be Aesopian! Be mindfully aware of the lessons and possible fables you may find in everyday living.
- Become a student of Aesop and his fables. I have given you the tools.
- Take the 30-day challenge and help someone, a client, a friend, a family member. Pick out a few fables and simply suggest they read them and ask for their feedback. Have a conversation.
- Go to www.magicofaesop.com for a few extra chapters.
- Buy a few good illustrated children's version of Aesop's Fables. A small investment and you'll have a handful to 'gift' to your client as part of their hypnotic change work journey.

Remember, throughout Aesop's life he strived to influence and teach the philosophers of his time, and the philosophy students and friends of his master, Xandrus. Aesop used his wit and wisdom to earn his freedom. Much in the same way, using Aesop's life as a metaphor with your clients, help them become free from their suffering, their paralysis and help them move forward in their life all by sharing a few ancient hypnotic stories.

Like Aesop, it's time for you to become the teacher.

Appendix A – Resources Consulted

Numerous works are referenced for this book, in no particular order but each invaluable. A special thank you goes to author Laura Gibbs, the Aesopian scholar for her enthusiastic support!

- *Aesopica: A Series of Texts Relating to Aesop or Ascribed to Him by Ben Edwin Perry*
  The most complete corpus of the proverbs and fables of Aesop ever assembled
- *The Legendary Life and Fables of Aesop,* edited by Mayvis Anthony
- *Aesop's Fables: A New Translation* by Laura Gibbs (Oxford World's Classics)
- *Vita Aesopi: The Life of Aesop* (Aesop Romances) by Maximus the Confessor, 1518
- *Aesop's Fables,* translated by George Fyler Townsend, 1887
- Project Gutenberg
- *The English Fable: Aesop and Literary Culture 1651 - 1740* by Jayne Lewis

- *My Voice Will Go with You: The Teaching Tales of Milton H. Erickson*
- *The Culture of Education* by Jerome Bruner
- Thich Nhat Hanh's *Enlightenment and Walking Meditations*
- *The Fables of Aesop,* as first printed by Wm Caxton, 1484, London
- *The Fables of Aesop,* edited by Joseph Jacobs with illustrations by Richard Heighway (1894).
- *The Romulus: Paraphrases of Phaedrus (1870)*
- *Mythologia Aesopica,* by Isaac Nevelet (1610)
- *The Fables of Jean de La Fontaine, 1668-1694,* by de La Fontaine
- Loeb Classical Library *Babrius and Phaedrus Fables*
- *The Fables of Aesop* illustrated by Edward Julius Detmold (1909)
- *An Argosy of Fables:* A Representative Selection from the Fable Literature of Every Land and Culture, and in the equally important book,
- *The Talking Beasts: A book of Fable Wisdom,* which presents fables from across world cultures.
- *The Life of Aesop,* commonly known as The Life in Aesopica circles.

Appendix B – Fables and Morals
(www.aesopfables.com)

FABLE	MORAL OF THE STORY
The Ant and the Chrysalis	Appearances are deceptive
The Ant and the Dove	One good turn deserves another
The Ant and the rasshopper	It is best to prepare for the days of necessity
The Ass and His Masters	He that finds discontentment in one place is not likely to find happiness in
The Ass and his Purchaser	A man is known by the company he keeps
The Ass in the Lion's Skin	Fine clothes may disguise, but silly words will disclose a fool
The Ass the Fox and the Lion	* Never trust your enemy
The Bald Man and the Fly	-Revenge will hurt the avenger-
The Bat the Birds and the Beasts	He that is neither one thing nor the other has no friends

FABLE	MORAL OF THE STORY
The Bear and the Two Travelers	Misfortune tests the sincerity of friends
The Bee and Jupiter	Evil wishes, like chickens, come home to roost
The Blind Man and the Whelp	Evil tendencies are shown in early life
The Boy and the Filberts	Do not attempt too much at once
The Boys and the Frogs	-One man's pleasure may be another's pain-
The Boy and the Nettles	Whatever you do, do with all your might
The Cat and Venus	Nature exceeds nurture
The Crow and the Pitcher	Necessity is the mother of invention
The Crow and the Pitcher	Little by little does the trick
The Dancing Monkeys	Not everything you see is what it appears to be-
The Dog and the Hare	No one can be a friend if you know not whether to trust or distrust him
The Dog in the Manger	Ah, people often grudge others what they cannot enjoy themselves
The Dogs and the Fox	It is easy to kick a man that is down
The Dog and the Wolf	Better starve free than be a fat slave
The Dove and the Ant	Little friends may prove great friends
The Eagle and the Arrow	We often give our enemies the means for our own destruction
The Eagle and the Fox	Do unto others as you would have them do unto you
The Eagle the Cat and the Wild Sow	Gossips are to be seen and not heard

FABLE	MORAL OF THE STORY
The Farmer and the Stork	Birds of a feather flock together
The Father and His Two Daughters	You can't please everybody
The Four Oxen and the Lion	United we stand, divided we fall
The Fox Who Had Lost His Tail	Misery loves company
The Fox and the Goat	Look before you leap
The Fox and the Grapes	It is easy to despise what you cannot get
The Fox and the Hedgehog	A needy thief steals more than one who enjoys plenty
The Frogs and the Well	Look before you leap
The Frogs Asking for King	Let well enough alone
The Frogs Desiring a King	Better no rule than cruel rule
The Goose with the Golden Eggs	Greed oft o'er reaches itself
The Hare and the Tortoise	Plodding wins the race
The Hares and the Frogs	There is always someone worse off than yourself
The Hare with Many Friends	He that has many friends, has no friends
The Hart and the Hunter	We often despise what is most useful to us
The Hart in the Ox-Stall	Nothing escapes the master's eye
The Heifer and the Ox	He laughs best that laughs last
Hercules and the Waggoner	The gods help them that help themselves

FABLE	MORAL OF THE STORY
The Horse and Groom	A man may smile yet be a villain
The Horse Hunter and Stag	If you allow men to use you for your own purposes, they will use you for
The Hunter and the Woodman	The hero is brave in deeds as well as words
The Jay and the Peacock	It is not only fine feathers that make fine birds
The Kid and the Wolf	If you must revile your neighbor, make certain first that he cannot reach
The Kings Son and the Painted Lion	We had better bear our troubles bravely than try to escape them
The Lion and the Eagle	Try before you trust
The Lion and the Mouse	Little friends may prove great friends
The Lion in Love	Even the wildest can be tamed by love
The Lion the Bear and the Fox	It sometimes happens that one man has all the toil, and another all the profit
The Lion's Share	You may share the labours of the great, but you will not share the spoil
The Man Bitten by a Dog	Benefits bestowed upon the evil-disposed increase their means of
The Man and the Satyr	Some men can blow hot and blow cold with the same breath
The Man the Boy and the Donkey	Please all, and you will please none
Mercury and the Woodman	Honesty is the best policy
The Milkmaid and Her Pail	Do not count your chickens before they are hatched
The Miller His Son and Their Ass	Try to please all and you end by pleasing none
The Miser	The true value of money is not in its possession but in its use

FABLE	MORAL OF THE STORY
The Monkey and the Dolphin	Those who pretend to be what they are not, sooner or later, find themselves in deep water
The Monkeys and Their Mother	The best intentions will not always ensure success
The Mule	Every truth has two sides
The Nurse and the Wolf	Enemies promises were made to be broken
The Old Woman and the Physician	He who plays a trick must be prepared to take a joke
The Old Woman and the Wine Jar	The memory of a good deed lives
The One-Eyed Doe	Trouble comes from the direction we least expect it
The Oxen and the Axle Trees	Those who suffer most cry out the least
The Peacock and the Crane	Fine feathers don't make fine birds
The Rose and the Amaranth	Greatness carries its own penalties
The Seagull and the Kite	Every man should be content to mind his own business
The Serpent and the Eagle	One good turn deserves another
The Serpent and the File	It is useless attacking the insensible
The Shepherds Boy and the Wolf	There is no believing a liar, even when he speaks the truth
The Shipwrecked Impostor	A liar deceives only himself
The Sick Stag	Evil companions bring more hurt than profit
The Swallow and the Crow	Fair weather friends are not worth much
The Thief and the Innkeeper	Every tale is not to be believed

FABLE	MORAL OF THE STORY
The Three Tradesmen	Every man for himself
The Vixen and the Lioness	Quality is better than quantity
The Wolf and the Kid	It is easy to be brave from a safe distance
The Wolf in Sheep's Clothing	Appearances are deceptive
The Woodman and the Serpent	No gratitude from the wicked

Aesop

He sat among the woods, he heard
The sylvan merriment; he saw
The pranks of butterfly and bird,
The humors of the ape, the daw.

And in the Honor the frog—
In all the life of moor and fen,
In ass and peacock, stork and log,
He read similitudes of men.

"Of these, from those," he cried, "we come
Our hearts, our brains descend from these.
And lo! the Beasts no more were dumb,
But answered out of brakes and trees;

"Not ours," they cried; "Degenerate,
If ours at all," they cried again,
Ye fools, who war with God and Fate,
Who strive and toil: strange race of men,

For we are neither bond nor free,
For we have neither slaves nor kings.
But near to Nature's heart are we,
And conscious of her secret things.

Content are we to fall asleep.
And well content to wake no more,
We do not laugh; we do not weep.
Nor look behind us and before;

But were there cause for moan or mirth,
'T is we, not you, should sigh or scorn.
Oh, latest children of the Earth
Most childish children Earth has borne.

They spoke, but that misshapen Slave
Told never of the thing he heard.
And unto men their portraits gave,
In likenesses of beast and bird!

A.L

About the Author

Robert Martel is a professional hypnotist, marketing writer, speaker and small business consultant. He is a popular seminar leader and corporate trainer and is the host of the weekly AM radio show, Mind Magic! Bob is the author of How to Create All of the Business You Can Handle: Smart Strategies for Small Business Owners. An aquanaut and an aeronaut, Bob is a veteran of the US Navy's Submarine Service, and he is a commercial hot-air balloon pilot. Intrigued by Aesop his entire life, he is anxious to share more about this legendary character who continues to influence the world. Connect with Bob at www.positiveresultshypnosis.com, www.magicofaesop.com or via email at bob@bobmartel.com

Made in the USA
Middletown, DE
22 March 2022